DATE		

Why Should Extroverts Make All the Money?

Networking

Made Easy for the Introvert

FREDERICA J. BALZANO, PH.D.
WITH MARSHA BOONE KELLY

CB
CONTEMPORARY BOOKS

Library of Congress Cataloging-in-Publication Data

Balzano, Frederica J.
    Why should extroverts make all the money? : networking
made easy for the introvert / Frederica J. Balzano with Marsha
Boone Kelly.
       p.   cm.
    ISBN 0-8092-2816-5
    1. Business networks.   2. Introversion.   I. Kelly, Marsha
Boone.   II. Title.
    HD69.S8B35   1999
    650.1'3—dc21   98-49521
                                        CIP

To Tracy Jo-Ann
And in memory of Christopher and Jerri Jr.

Cover design by Scott Rattray
Interior design by City Desktop Productions, Incorporated

Published by Contemporary Books
A division of NTC/Contemporary Publishing Group, Inc.
4255 West Touhy Avenue, Lincolnwood (Chicago), Illinois 60646-1975 U.S.A.
Copyright © 1999 by Frederica J. Balzano, Ph.D.
Printed in the United States of America
International Standard Book Number: 0-8092-2816-5
99 00 01 02 03 04 MV 15 14 13 12 11 10 9 8 7 6 5 4 3 2 1

CONTENTS

ACKNOWLEDGMENTS

To Sandi Carroll, a researcher extraordinaire; to everyone at NTC/Contemporary Publishing, especially Kara Leverte; to Mark Taylor, who saw the big picture when he read the proposal; and to Agnes Birnbaum, my literary agent, who suggested this book. For all of her nurturing and attentiveness during the long months, I offer my heartfelt thanks.

INTRODUCTION

Frequently, introverts are untapped gold mines of creativity, offering many contributions but often waiting to be recognized—especially in the workplace, which is the general focus of this book. *Why Should Extroverts Make All the Money?* speaks to the millions of introverted people who have too often been dismissed as shy (a different personality trait that will be discussed later), passive, arrogant, or just uninterested in whatever is happening around them. Actually, introverts rarely fit these categories. But for introverts in the workplace, it's more important than ever to recognize others' perceptions of their behavior.

One reason is because the old idea of remaining with one company for a lifetime, then retiring with the proverbial gold watch and comfortable pension, is just that: old. Corporate downsizing has been the trend in the 1990s. During the decade we saw Ma Bell (AT&T) severely cut its middle-management staff. Big Blue (IBM) also dismissed workers by the thousands and sold its corporate headquarters. This has become the norm. During the same period, the *New York Times* ran a week-long series on the ongoing downsizing of corporate America, specifically devoted to those companies that had reduced their staffs by a few hundred to several thousand (1996 March 3–9).

It's little wonder then that the refrains of career seminars have become: "Build your contact list!" "Let people know about your skills!" "Meet new people!" and "Explore new avenues of opportunity!" All of these opportunities are found through *networking*.

Secondly, we no longer live in a society where people manufacture and market "widgets." The whole concept of going into a factory and screwing a bolt into a hole is over. We now market services. We market intellect. We market technology. We have seen the end of the Industrial Revolution. That world does not exist anymore. The cotton gin and the plow moved us away from hunting and gathering. Technology is taking us to places we never dreamed about. From our homes, we can use computers, modems, faxes, and teleconferencing equipment, conducting international business—and "still not take a shower," as the commercial tells us. Business has evolved and operates at the cutting edge of the technological revolution.

People get paid for ideas and concepts—not necessarily for immediate productivity. Also, individuals in the workforce now have unlimited variety in the type of work they do. The new buzzword, "You, Inc.," increasingly applies. *You* are now a product, and as a product *you* must go out and market yourself. Therefore, as we will see, the networking process has become the solution to attaining a new and ostensibly "improved" you.

It's a Small World After All

I had a mentor several years ago who used to tell me there were only four hundred people in the world, and sooner or later we would all meet one another. This story is one of many that I love to tell people:

Way out on the eastern end of Long Island in New York, I met a woman named Maria. During our banter I asked her whether she was a "local" or a "recent"; she replied that she was originally from Vermont. It turned out she was from a town called Killington, near where my daughter had spent all of her early childhood and adolescent years going to a summer camp. Then, Maria said her mom was the postmaster for the area and delivered mail to that camp—so her mom had delivered my letters to my daughter! As my mentor said, we're all connected!

One of the characters in *Six Degrees of Separation*, a Broadway play that later became a movie, claimed that everyone is linked by a remarkably small number of relationships. Nearly all of us have discovered a common acquaintance through a stranger who strikes up a conversation with us (since it is rare that we introverts "cast the first stone").

In a segment of *Morning Edition* on National Public Radio, reporter David Barron interviewed Duncan Watts, a mathematics researcher at Manhattan College University in New York, who talked about the concept of the six degrees of separation. This theory originates from a few very simple calculations done by social scientists in the 1950s and 1960s. They discovered that we are connected to everyone else in the world through a series of only six people.

Watts explained this phenomenon as follows. "Assume that you have a thousand acquaintances and each of them has a thousand different acquaintances: one thousand times one thousand equals one million second-order acquaintances. And at three degrees of separation, you have somewhere on the order of one billion. And then, very quickly, you start to encompass the whole world," (1998 June 4).

Watts and Steven Strogatz, of Cornell University, used a computer simulation to map the relationship of everyone on earth to everyone else by using a surrogate network: that of movie actors.

In the popular game called "Six Degrees of Kevin Bacon," players try to link up any film actor to the actor Kevin Bacon through intermediary steps. Take Charlie Chaplin, for instance: "Charlie Chaplin was in *A Countess from Hong Kong* in 1967 with Marlon Brando. Marlon Brando was in *Apocalypse Now*, made in 1979, with Laurence Fishburne, who was in *Quicksilver* in 1986 with Kevin Bacon. That's three links. We then say: Charlie Chaplin has a Bacon number of three," (1998 June 4). So Watts and Strogatz suggest, in fact, that you and I, the president of the United States, and a gondolier in Venice may be no more than four or five degrees of separation apart.

Christopher E. Kelley, author of *How to Be a Star at Work* (1998), says that we all have the ability to become just like the stars of Hollywood, and the secret is in networking and the way things get done. "Stars" do this all of the time. They are always on the lookout for people to add to their network. When they find themselves in a meeting that's a waste of time—and we all have too many meetings like that every day—they use the time to identify people in the meeting who are worth getting to know.

In a 1997 interview, LaFaye Baker, a Hollywood stuntwoman, revealed one of the most challenging areas of her job that calls for her diligent attention: "Networking and politicking, because that's what this business is all about. You have to find your own work. We don't have agents, so I have to send out pictures and resumes, contact the stunt coordinators for a film or TV show, be on the sets, hang out and shoot the breeze with people in the industry. It's an up-and-down business," (Edwards 1997).

No matter *what* business we're in, sooner or later we will all have to find *and create* our own work. And we'll have to go out and market ourselves.

Extroverts love this whole process; introverts may find it daunting. Extroverts find joy in meeting new people, whereas introverts can feel slightly intimidated. Even after they realize that 75 percent of all new opportunities lie with new contacts, most introverts rank meeting new people right up there with getting a root canal.

Why Should Extroverts Make All the Money? can alleviate the networking pain for introverts. This book offers help in three main ways: by providing information (for everyone) about introversion, and its *value*; by presenting techniques to help introverted and shy people identify and excel in suitable jobs and to successfully approach (and conquer) networking; and, finally, by explaining introverted management methods that foster communication between managers and their staff. *Why Should Extroverts Make All the Money?* will demonstrate how to know, understand, and appreciate the dynamic qualities of introverts—so they can contribute their maximum abilities to what has become an increasingly diverse and enriched workforce.

Why This Book?

In my business as an executive career coach and management consultant, I have assessed hundreds of introverted adults. Over time, I have learned that it is often our personality or personality conflicts that interfere with our ability to get ahead in the work environment. How often do we hear, "It's not what you know, it's *who* you know" or "Being liked by the *right* people will help you reach success?" Well, people who frequently and comfortably engage in social conversations, and have invigorating personalities, generally do get to know more people and are often more well-liked. Introverts, on the other hand, sometimes get overlooked for promotions—while those who are more aggressive and gregarious are the people who get selected to rise up the ranks of the corporate ladder. Introverts often create the impression that they are aloof or uninterested, when in reality they may simply prefer to be observers rather than players. Left to themselves, introverts are often content to remain on the sidelines.

But today's mean-and-lean workplace requires everyone to be an active and intensely enterprising contributor to the bottom line. Introverts, therefore, must recognize their own value and also learn how to play the game in order to get ahead or at least to stay comfortable where they're at.

Why Should Extroverts Make All the Money? is a compilation of methods that work—actual tools extroverts have long used to succeed. Absorbing case histories, including my own, provide platforms for in-depth discussions and further clarify personality types and behavior, strategic business and career management, networking, and finding personal business fulfillment.

Audience

The audience for *Why Should Extroverts Make All the Money?* includes the millions of people who have had, and may experience, difficulty functioning optimally as a result of their introverted personalities. This includes introverts within large corporations; owners of small businesses; and middle and senior managers. Small or individual business owners caught between the need to deliver a product or service and their inability to "work" the market will find this book particularly useful.

Introverts, like others who have been passively hating their jobs, complaining about their boss, cursing the direction of their company, being offered a buyout, fearing future employment prospects—fear no more. The tools introverts need to take charge of their careers (and even their lives) can be found in this book.

Why Should Extroverts Make All the Money? also teaches introverted managers to deliver powerful ideas at meetings, unchallenged, and gain greater strength to lead. Extroverted managers will learn to listen and motivate *all* employees more effectively.

Women, in particular, can benefit from *Why Should Extroverts Make All the Money?* because historically, women, especially those of the baby boom generation, were told that they did not have to develop effective networking skills; that, as communicators, they were not as good as men; that they were prone to excessive emotion and wouldn't be able to get men to either listen to, or follow, their ideas. For women, the glass ceiling continues to exist, perpetuated by these stereotypes, but *Why Should Extroverts Make All the Money?* can help women drive another crack into it.

My Experience with Networking

I score very high on tests for introversion—but I have also managed to comfortably tackle public speaking and to interact with large groups of people. I have also skillfully developed other traits needed to succeed in many professions today. Managing my own business, Effective Management Resources, Inc., a strategic management consulting firm, makes it mandatory for me to stay totally in step with all aspects and functions of networking. We are dedicated to assisting human resource professionals with the techniques to develop the right people with the right skills in the right job, thereby maintaining an effective, productive, and committed workforce. I manage a comprehensive, professional staff, and our expertise lies in leadership development, executive assessment and coaching, career management and transition counseling, and improving company diversity plans.

Our winning Networking for Introverts program, the only seminar of its kind in the market, has been hailed as a first in its field for effecting real change for individuals and organizations as they interface with today's changing business environments. Heavily researched, Networking for Introverts explores the myths of introversion and gives participants a model to usein becoming more effective in an extroverted workforce. This increases their own, as well as their organization's, effectiveness.

In our executive coaching model, we work with high-potential executives who may need development in one or more career-management areas, or individual coaching around issues related to working with a diverse workforce. The focus of this program is to help participants achieve and maintain excellent work performance within the complexities of organizational change. Our clients confirm their current career direction, consider possible new directions, or find ways to improve a job that has become routine or is just no longer a good fit. The executive coaching is typically tailored to the needs of mid-level employees wishing to join the senior managerial team.

Executive coaching is also effectively used with survivors of downsizing, restructuring, mergers, and acquisitions—those who are faced with the issues of effectively managing a career in a new environment. Whether your goal is targeted for senior management or not, *Why Should Extroverts Make All the Money?* has invaluable information for everyone—in and outside of business. During the earlier part of my professional working life, I never heard of an executive coach. I hope that *my* personal "networking as an introvert" story and the captivating stories of my clients that follow will help you appreciate the personal and professional benefits of networking.

I love my job as a consultant, but I have to admit that writing this book has been one of the joys of my life, because I got to do lots and lots of research, sit in my office and think, and, best of all, write. These are tasks I treasure and do best.

In fact, networking is one of the most difficult things that I have *ever* had to do.

Many years ago Jack Benny did a skit in which he was accosted by a robber. The robber demanded, "Your money or your life?" Benny got that very blank stare on his face. The robber was becoming impatient. He repeated, "Your money or your life?" "I'm thinking, I'm thinking," Benny replied. That was how I felt when a colleague first asked me, "Would you network if your life depended on it?" I thought about it and finally I said, "No." Of course I was joking, but there are days I really feel that way. It has been far easier to teach others these tools and techniques than for me to implement them myself.

Contrary to what many who know me probably think, networking does not come easily to me. I think I am of the "I know how to do it, but I just really don't want to do it" school. Many times, *I* have had to script out my phone calls before I picked up the phone. I need to ask myself: who is this person who will be on the other end of the line, how can they help me, and what do I need most from them?

As I've said, I manage my own business, so if I don't pick up the phone, my consultants and I will all starve to death. But networking is not about making cold calls; it's OK for us to leave that to the salespeople. My business depends on relationships, and I have learned over the years that I build relationships very well. That is my strength, and we capitalize on it. But how did all of this come about?

Many years ago, when I worked in the world of not-for-profit organizations, I decided to make a career change. I wanted to try working in the private sector, but I was told, "No way!"

Do you realize that some people in your life can be toxic? Whatever it is that you want to do, they give you one hundred reasons why it can't be done. Well, I was told that the world of not-for-profit organizations and the private sector were like oil and water. I was also told that folks in the private sector don't like or trust academics: "They think that you think you're smarter than they are."

Well, I actually began to do some networking, although I did not realize that that was what it was called. I went around and spoke to people I was told to speak with. But I did it without a pitch. No one told me I was supposed to have one, or what it even was. And I was not clear about the things I had to offer the private sector. For that matter, I was also not clear about what corporations did! I babbled a lot, and I lost the few contacts I had. I did not know how to follow up. I never did any research. And it did not work. Not only did it not work, I think I probably made some people quite confused and angry. I was really clueless about the entire networking process.

Then, continuing to plod along in the dark, down the networking path, I had what could have been a wonderful contact at Catalyst, an organization in New York City that works with women's issues. I could have *merged* my research skills with my not-for-profit background within a corporate structure. Instead, I called them up out of the blue and actually got the president of the organization on the phone. "What do you want to do?" she curiously asked. And I said, "I don't know." Then the conversation bumbled on like that for a painful few minutes. Finally, she said I should go polish up my pitch, and she hung up on me. I was angry and humiliated. I felt she should have seen me and hired me. But for what? To do what? I suppose the rational part of me really knew I had blown it.

I had quite a setback and it actually took me another couple of years before I would try the process again. But this time, I was armed with some techniques. I used my background in assessment and teaching to network into the human resources training and outplacement departments. I had a very good friend who helped me build a winning resume. I had a better idea of what I wanted to do. I even developed a pitch. This time I was far more successful. I landed a consulting assignment in a major financial institution, where we helped employees in downsized departments find new jobs. It was my turn to help others . . . and get *paid* at the same time.

Life was good!

With Help from a Friend

The other writer of this book, Marsha Boone Kelly, has been working with me since the beginning of the project when we wrote the book's proposal. Using much creativity and skill, Marsha wrote various sections of the manuscript and did the overall melding and editing. She also contributed to the creation of chapter titles, headings, and the very title of the book itself.

A native New York City resident, Marsha attended Central State University, graduated from Long Island University, and did graduate work at NYU. Since leaving her career in higher education, she's been a proposal writer for nonprofit organizations, written about business strategies for the Career Management section of *Black Enterprise,* and worked at Prodigy Company and *Money* magazine. Currently, she works in the Lifestyle department at *Essence* magazine and is the Careers editor of *Essence Online.*

During the past year, I gave Marsha one of the personality-type-indicator assessment tools that I use to help determine where *she* falls on the introvert/extrovert curve. As I suspected, it turns out that she is mostly extroverted with decisive introverted traits, leaving her very near the middle of the scale.

Marsha, too, shares a portion of her professional and personal experiences in this book.

Finally, the Truth About Introverts and Their Power

"You can observe a lot by watching."

Yogi Berra

Counter to popular beliefs, introverts do not sit in the dark and just contemplate our existence (well, not all of the time anyway). We manage jobs, families, and all of life's other responsibilities.

Introverts do not, out of necessity, wear black or other fade-into-the-woodwork colors. And we are not boring—ok, sometimes we are boring, but so are lots of other people (like some extroverts who love to hear themselves talk). Introverts are not all computer techies and number crunchers either, though we do tend to gravitate toward such careers. Introverts *are* reflective thinkers and the world's conceptualizers. We focus on analysis and inner communication.

Our ever-evolving society needs a conscious understanding of human beings, their purpose, and how that purpose may be fulfilled. For individuals, this understanding can be achieved through contemplative self-analysis, as part of a personal self-discovery process. We must ask ourselves: "Who am I? What is the goal of my life? What are my unique contributions?" Problems and conflicts (business conflicts included) can open the door to opportunities for growth, increased self-awareness, and positive change. Such an approach to conflict resolution or business-related problem solving, for example, can initially be inner directed. And people committed to inner growth and development readily promote and conduct themselves through positive approaches to their affairs and lives, bringing more order and balance into the environment around them.

But it's also not unusual to find introverts, shy people, and others unaware of their inner strengths. And being self-conscious, introverts sometimes fail to relax, open up, take risks, and truly thrive.

Also, we all have certain fears. "Often fear stands between man and his perfect self-expression. Stage-fright has hampered many a genius," (Shinn 1925). As we overcome fear and lose all of our negative self-consciousness, we become fearless and more confident. Through conscious effort, which will be demonstrated in later chapters, we can train ourselves and practice the act of stepping outside (what we perceive to be) our personal "safety zones."

As more introverted individuals realize their natural strengths, they will expand all areas relating to positive self-development, self-awareness, and thus, those unique contributions.

Expanded inner growth and development will lead to further involvement with new forms of work-related values, and society will benefit from a more innovative and flexible workforce. Thus, people who are highly self-aware have, and can *offer to society*, a gift.

Introverts, who tend to spend much of their time reflecting on their inner thoughts, often devise new ideas and strategies. (The *really* lucky ones hire extroverts to carry them out.)

And with regular periods of introspection and silent contemplation, people in general may experience less difficulty in maintaining a healthy work and lifestyle pace and balance. It's all about positive-directed awareness, knowing yourself, realizing your individual strengths, setting comfortable goals, being self-confident, acting on your beliefs, and—through networking—cultivating yourself for success and implementing the goals you set. If you are an introvert, this means cultivating your introverted personality and lifestyle for the success you desire.

Picture yourself strolling along the well-worn path of your life into the woods. The woods are dark, and except for a distant glow of light that comes from a place beyond the trail, you see only images and shadows. The trail has a handrail that you grasp for security.

Grabbing this rail has obvious advantages: You don't get scratched by bushes and brambles, you don't trip on unseen roots and vines, and, above all, you don't get lost in the woods. But staying on the beaten path has a big downside too: You can go only where the trail leads you and the largest part of the forest remains inaccessible. You learn nothing about the lore of the woods, or about survival, by walking a narrow path, and you have little evidence that the path goes anywhere except in a circle.

Every so often the trail washes out. This will happen throughout your life, often in unexpected ways: the loss of a job, a forced relocation, a divorce, a serious illness, a new love, the birth of a child, or sudden and unexpected success. You can't escape stress even when you have been holding onto the rail for dear life.

As you move along the beaten path, you become aware of the rumblings of distant drums calling from mysterious places. Although the darkness looks worrisome, your curiosity and desire beckon you, so you let go of the rail and walk toward a promising new set of experiences.

Like many before you, you let go of the rail with apprehension only to discover that you can see more than before. Because of this, you feel a sensation of giddy liberation. Nonetheless, when you meet your first big challenge, you may feel like a butterfly in a hurricane. You long to return to the security of the well-worn path. Yet by sticking it out—learning to learn, adapting to change—you empower yourself to go forward.

You break from the rail when you test your skills in different ways. The shy person who (now) socializes develops confidence. The procrastinator who gets organized discovers an inner drive for closure. The impulsive person who learns to reflect develops tolerance. Through this process, you command your finest attributes.

Changing paths involves some risk. The path you are on might be the very place you want to be. The new direction you choose can exclude other opportunities. Yet, when you feel as if you are going around in circles, prudent risks are normally worth taking. There is another reason to break from the rail. Looking back on their lives, most people regret what they did *not* dare to do more than they regret the errors they made. Those who rarely risk anything have the most to regret. (Knaus 1994*)

Change Your Life Now by Dr. William J. Knaus, copyright ©1994 by Dr. William J. Knaus. Reprinted by permission of John Wiley & Sons, Inc.

While out for dinner one evening with a friend, I talked about writing a seminar specifically for introverts. I told her I felt I was the perfect person to write this since I am highly introverted and have long observed that introverts are often overlooked, taken for granted, or undervalued. She looked at me with an astonished expression. Her response was that I could not possibly be an introvert. Why not? Because I had a great sense of humor, and I wore red fingernail polish. "Introverts," she said, "live in basements inventing new computer programs for the destruction of the universe as we know it."

"That," I told her, "is dysfunction—not introversion." But it did start me thinking. If a really good friend reacted to the news that I was an introvert as if I had told her I had a life-threatening illness, how must the rest of the world view us? This question prompted *this* introvert to take a closer look at the multifaceted lives of introverts. Case histories from my files showed how some introverts overcame business-related conflicts and challenges in a variety of situations. These successful individuals learned how to *change their paths*. Built into these case studies is helpful "how-to" advice for introverts. The following chapters include examples of entrepreneurs, small-business owners, and assorted professionals—all introverts who were told they couldn't be fruitful in marketing their services and products.

Louis, for example, who consulted me several years ago, is a very successful surgeon at a premier hospital in New York City. But in his middle age, he found himself feeling hungry. For what? He didn't know! His family and friends were amazed by his professional and personal achievements. What more could he possibly have wanted out of his life? But he really felt that something was missing. He was not fulfilled.

We worked very well together. We knew he was an introvert, but as he completed his assessment and wrote his "autobiography" exercise (see Chapter 8), we discovered that becoming a doctor was not *his* choice of career. He became a doctor because his mother wanted him to be a doctor! Then she could tell all her friends in the old neighborhood about her son, "the doctor." Classic, but true.

What did Louis really want as a career? Well, from his assessment we acknowledged that he loved film. He loved creating. And he loved getting people to pay attention to his work. Louis wanted to be Steven Spielberg!

Now, Louis could hardly be expected to give up a lucrative medical career to become a top Hollywood producer. How would he continue to pay his mortgage? What to do?

Well, Louis first spoke to people in the film industry. He found that not a lot of people made a great living from it, but they loved what they did.

He then researched production companies that did work in the medical field. He looked into up-and-coming companies involved in animation and found a very successful one in the Midwest. He visited them with his idea, which was to produce films using animation for patients who were about to undergo surgery. Louis wanted to make films that would be fun to watch for people who were apprehensive about what lay ahead. He hired actors who sounded caring and concerned to do voice-overs. And he launched his own company, a company that is still in existence today—and very successful, I might add.

Louis found a niche that combined his technical expertise with his passion for visuals. Throughout this book you will read about such success stories, and learn how *you* can be successful as well. As Louis went on to develop his flourishing small video company devoted to making innovative and creative films that teach and inform patients about their upcoming surgery, many others have found their calling or a more compatible fit—and, for them, a better, more suitable way to live.

Another interesting situation involves the case of lawyers (pardon the pun). Case studies show that many lawyers, although extremely successful in school, find themselves searching for a career change when faced with marketing their new firm and logging billable hours. The law school environment nurtures the introvert. After all, students spend immense portions of their time quietly reading and researching in libraries. But large law firms insist that their senior associates and partners bring in business, creating a kind of schizophrenia for introverted lawyers. Few firms will hire (and keep) a "quiet, reserved" lawyer. A perfect example of this concept is the contrasting styles of defense attorney Johnnie Cochran, the flashy extrovert, and prosecuting attorney Christopher Darden, the conservative introvert (I'm making an assumption here for the purpose of showing contrast), during the O. J. Simpson trial.

Steve, a client of mine and an attorney, was forced by his firm to consider a change. He reached a crossroads in his career when he was asked to either become a partner or leave the firm. Steve decided to start his own small law firm.

Steve and the "wanna-be Steven Spielberg" are good examples of how introverts can use their natural talents and assets to establish their desired goals. And with cultivation and a certain amount of risk, you too can experience more fulfillment and achieve greater success.

2

THE DIFFERENCE BETWEEN INTROVERSION AND SHYNESS

"We have deep depth."

YOGI BERRA

The year was 1975. Men were in polyester shirts unbuttoned to mid-chest and women were in platform heels and slinky dresses grooving to Donna Summer as a glittering ball revolved above the dance floor like everyone's personal North Star. This was the dawn of the disco era and the image that was (and today, socially, often still is) indelibly engraved said: Life is a party. And the guest lists at these affairs included smiling men and women self-confident enough to get out on the dance floor and "boogie on down." (Carducci and Zimbardo 1995)

But, was this, or is this, the life that everyone lives?
Why Should Extroverts Make All the Money? is designed to help the introvert as well as the person who considers himself

9

or herself to be shy. But what's the difference? Well, I could get really psychological about it, but the details would also be confusing, clinical, and boring. That's not what this book is about. But the following little glossary, from Stanford University psychologist Philip Zimbardo, Ph.D., one of the authors of the opening passage and an expert on shyness, explains some of the differences:

- **Extroversion:** A personal preference for socially engaging activities and settings.

- **Introversion:** A personal preference for solitary, non-social activities and settings.

- **Shy Extrovert:** A person who performs well socially but experiences painful thoughts and feelings (Henderson and Zimbardo 1998).

Metaphorically, shyness is a shrinking back from life that weakens the bonds of human connection.

In his bestselling book, *Shyness*, Zimbardo describes a shy person as someone who is "inhibited from acting because of inner commands: 'You'll look ridiculous; people will laugh at you; this is not the place to do that; I won't allow you the liberty to be spontaneous; do not raise your hand, volunteer, dance, sing or make yourself obvious; you'll be safe only if you're not seen and not heard.' And the prisoner-within decides not to risk the 'dangerous' freedom of spontaneous life, and meekly complies" (1977, 3).

In a conversation I had with Dr. Zimbardo in 1996 concerning the distinction between shyness and introversion, he told me, "Shyness adds to anxiety. Shy people want to be with others, but can't. Introverts, on the other hand, may have anxieties, but not necessarily as a result of their introversion. And a distinctive difference between shyness and introversion is that introversion is a conscious choice." Research has distinguished shyness from introversion, although they are typically related. Introverts simply prefer solitary to social activities (but do not fear social encounters as do the shy), while extroverts prefer social to solitary activities. Although the majority of people that are shy are introverted, shy extroverts are found in many behavioral settings. They are privately shy and publicly outgoing. They have the requisite social skills and can carry them out flawlessly in highly structured, scripted situations where everyone is playing prescribed roles and there is little room for spontaneity.

However, for the purpose of encouraging you to experience the networking process, I am treating introverts, shy folks, and shy extroverts equally. (I am focusing on being an equal opportunity writer!)

Why is it important to focus on introverts and shy people at all? Because Carducci and Zimbardo (1995) revealed that 40 percent of 800 American college students surveyed classified themselves as shy. The incidence of shyness in the United States may now be as high as 48 percent—and rising. According to Carducci and Zimbardo, this is partly due to the increased U.S. populations of traditionally modest cultures that condone more shy types of behavior.

Shy Extroverts

As mentioned, many people can be assessed as extroverts but consider themselves truly shy. They have learned how to behave as if they are outgoing, but this does not change their inner selves. These shy extroverts may have double personas. In public, they don't appear to be shy at all and can function quite well socially—but privately they are suffering, because they think a bunch of nonpositive things about themselves.

On the other hand, an introvert is an introvert is an introvert. Introverts can be extroverts when necessary, but the *type* remains consistent. An analogy to this is hair texture. The hair we're born with can be a shade of brown or blond. Or it can be a hue of red or almost black. It can be thick or thin and straight, curly, or kinky. The basic characteristics of our hair do not change, but we *can* alter its appearance. That becomes our choice. And an introvert can make a choice to behave like an extrovert.

Many celebrities and stand-up comedians in the entertainment industry are shy but adopt public personas. And although being shy can run the gamut from discomfort at a cocktail party to agoraphobia, in business, it is *never* good to be shy. Shyness in business is *always* negative. People who are introverted, however, often function well in the extroverted business environment because they can work at being extroverted when the situation calls for it. It is reported that talk-show host David Letterman, comedian Carol Burnett, and even television reporter Barbara Walters, are—you guessed it—shy extroverts. Shy extroverts in other careers, like educators and even politicians, have learned to act unreserved and unrestrained as long as they remain in their controlled environment. All types of shy people, however, share a common denominator: they are acutely self-conscious.

So, though introverts can, in certain circumstances, comfortably function, they should beware of situations in which they are competing with a particularly vivacious extrovert. The introverted tendency may be to sit back and allow the extrovert to openly rejoice and prevail. Extroverts assert and freely express themselves—without even trying—in all situations. Such was the case when I was the keynote speaker at an early morning conference in the fall of 1996.

A woman introduced herself to me and handed me her card. She told me who she was, what industry she was in (pub-

lishing), how she happened to be at this particular conference, how many grown children she had, what career each of
them was in, how she had managed to take the morning off
to attend this conference, and what she perceived was wrong
with her particular industry. It was only *8 A.M.* and I was trying to review my notes and find some coffee. During our conversation, since she was in the publishing industry, I told her
about the book I was writing on introversion. "But you're not
an introvert," she said. "Oh, but I am," said I. (Here we go
again!) "But," she asked, "we've been talking all this time—
how could you possibly be an introvert?"

Well, *we* had *not* been talking all this time—*she* had been
talking all this time. She was unaware that she had given me
far more information concerning her life than I needed to
know—and I, in true introverted fashion, had given her
absolutely no information about mine. And her perception of
an introvert was skewed toward someone who is very shy.

But had this been an interview, and she'd been the interviewer and I the interviewee, I would not have scored any
points with her at all; after she had a chance to think about
our meeting, she would not have had any sense about who I
was, or what my thoughts were. Also, again in true introverted
style, I might have been so delighted that she was doing all of
the talking, I could have allowed her to go on and on and on
while I imaginatively took a swim in the soothing emerald-
colored waters of Tahiti. In another scenario, if this lively
extrovert and I were interviewing for the same job, I could,
again, by comparison, have been perceived as the less appealing candidate—by not offering the interviewer enough information about myself and not giving enough *of* myself for them
to "like" me (and choose me). These two types of interview
situations can be extremely detrimental for the introvert who
is unaware.

Early Lives of Introverts

Looking back, many of us who consider ourselves introverts were probably considered shy as children. Although many children lose their shyness in time, others remain shy all their lives. And for a youngster who is shy, something like the first day of school, for example, can be extremely traumatic.

Do you remember the days when you had to be forced to go out to play—you did your homework first, then read or watched TV, and then *maybe* joined your friends? Introverts who never progress beyond this stage—who don't become more socially acclimated—are bound to have problems interacting with others as an adult.

When I was a practicing school psychologist, I often did research on separation anxiety in young children. The first day of school was always problematic for young children (especially four- and five-year-olds) who had difficulty leaving their parents. Many times the parents (usually the mothers) felt as guilty for leaving their children as the children were terrified of letting go. One of the ways to solve the battle of children being able to leave parents, and vice versa, was to invite new students into the school a few days before the official school opening in September. The children were able to meet with their teachers, explore the new environment, play with the toys, learn the location of the bathrooms, the kitchen, the bus stop, the music room, and so on. Thus, when school began, they were entering a familiar place, rather than a seemingly hostile and frightening environment.

We can apply this solution in our adult lives. Some introverts hate to travel—either to another corporate site within the city or across the world. Why? Traveling involves new business environments, new people, new conference rooms. It helps to bring a familiar picture of your family or friends from your office to place in your hotel room, just as you brought your favorite teddy bear to school. Or bring your favorite teddy bear! Listen, whatever works—*I* won't tell! If there is time (which there rarely is), first drive past the site where you will be meeting. Try to become as familiar as you can with the new environment.

Remember Psychology 101? Childhood is when we all begin to learn to negotiate: Who goes first? Was Julie out or safe at first base? Whose doll is that? Will you help me build castles in the sandbox? and so forth and so on. Whether shy or introverted, if you had problems within these early play groups, it's going to be tough for you to function on the job. Organizations function very much like your early play groups. There are always those chosen to be leaders—and then there's everyone else. Many millions of dollars are spent by companies to develop leaders. The extroverts will be out there throwing sand at you and moving ahead. They will be labeled as "high potentials." But quietly, in your own introverted style, you too can become a leader.

Shyness and the Many, Many Social Scenes of Adulthood

A shy person who is invited to a party tends to respond with apprehension. Chances are, you won't see them confidently "getting down" on the sparkling and enchanting dance floor. The shy person typically thinks, "I can't go. I don't know what to wear. I can't dance. People will stare at me." Shyness in its extreme sense can cause excessive fear and anxiety—and shy people may adopt especially unhealthy responses, such as excessive drinking, to alleviate or mask their uneasiness.

When a shy person is invited to speak at a meeting, to give a presentation, to be noticed or to gain exposure, these same anxieties may arise. Many clients have asked me, in all seriousness, if they should have a drink before going on an important interview. As destructive as that may sound, the client is entertaining the idea that it would be better to be more relaxed than to have all their faculties available. Of course the answer is "No, no, no!" This is where shyness can present even more difficulties.

If you consider my earlier premise about public and private personas, you will see that many entertainers *are* basically shy and cannot interact with people unless they are in the spotlight or have a script to follow. And some do latch on to the escapist route of excessive drinking and drugs, for various reasons. The anxiety of being constantly in the public eye, though, can be one contributing factor to some of the abusive lifestyles we all hear about in show business.

Most introverts do not believe people are going to laugh at them at a party, nor do they have major anxiety attacks about meeting the public. But they'd probably prefer to stay home and watch *Oprah* or *ER*—not to mention those old classic movies or more recent television reruns. The operative word here is *choice*. Introversion can be a preferred form of behavior.

3

Who Are You?

A Profile to Help Determine Whether You Are an Introvert

"You start chasing a ball and your brain immediately commands your body to 'run forward! Bend! Scoop up the ball! Peg it to the infield!' Then your body says 'who me?'"

Joe DiMaggio

If you think you're an introvert but have been feeling apprehensive because you don't realize that you truly have a gift, I wrote this book to tell you that you are not alone. Millions of adults feel the same way. I also wrote this book for the extroverts who can't quite figure out how to relate to or appreciate the introverts in their lives. In Chapter 6, Managing Introverts, I present helpful hints for working with the introvert who may have terrific ideas but lacks the ability to express them. Or you may feel that your spouse, significant other, or child might be more successful "if only he or she were less introverted." This book, therefore, is helpful for both introverts and extroverts.

So how do you know if you're an introvert? Here are some clues:

- Are you often asked, after a particularly long meeting, why you have been quieter than everyone else—if you're feeling all right?

- Are there times when you don't feel quite "with it" when you're in a large group of people?

- Does your mind sometimes wander during staff meetings?

Aha! Are you familiar with these patterns?

The following carefully constructed thirty-question quiz will superficially indicate your introverted status, the level of introversion, or whether you are an introvert at all.

Quiz: Are You an Introvert?

(Answer *Yes*, *Often*, or *No*)

1. In a large group, do you dislike introducing people to each other?

2. Do you prefer having only a few friends with whom you share intimate thoughts?

3. When you are with people, do you remain silent, keeping your thoughts to yourself?

4. In the office or other work environment, do you think you are perceived as being aloof by your coworkers?

5. Do you want to participate in meetings but are not sure how to start?

6. Do you think those close to you don't really know you or how you feel about most things?

7. Do you tend to daydream in meetings, thinking you've heard everyone's points before?

8. Do you find that you can rarely speak comfortably to almost anyone for as long as you have to?

9. Do you dread the thought of going to a cocktail party?

10. Are you uncomfortable "working the crowd" at a party?

11. Are few new acquaintances able to determine your interests right away?

12. When you are in a large group and everyone appears to be having a good time, do you find that you're bored?

13. Do acquaintances frequently ask if you're OK when you're feeling fine?

14. When in a large group of really enthusiastic friends, do you often find yourself feeling tired?

15. Have you heard close friends say that you're difficult to get to know?

16. Do you feel that your so-called shyness is standing in the way of career advancement?

17. Do you prefer to stay home, watching your favorite classic movie yet again on your VCR or curling up with a good book, rather than go to a party?

18. Are you mistrustful of people you meet for the first time?

19. Can you feel detached from friends who are having a good time?

20. Do you find that during the workday you need to close your office door and stare into space for several minutes, or take a walk around the block by yourself?*

21. Do you have to write notes before a presentation even if you don't refer to them, because you know you don't like to "wing" it?

22. When on a business trip, do you feel uncomfortable in your new surroundings?

23. When faced with a new project or problem, do you prefer to "go inside" your own thought processes rather than ask people for advice?

24. Do you feel that most people talk too much and think too little?

25. Do you feel pressure on the job to come up with answers prematurely?

26. Does the word *networking* send chills up your spine?

27. Would you prefer an iced bath over making a "cold call" to someone you do not know?

28. Is rejection so distasteful to you that it prevents you from effectively managing or networking?

29. Would you prefer to be perceived as a terrific leader rather than a good manager?

30. Does the thought of taking a two-week cruise with good friends leave you feeling frigid?

*Although introverts may like to do this, it is quite healthy for everyone.

Now tally your answers. If you responded "yes" or "often" to more than fifteen of these questions, you have a strong tendency toward introversion. If you answered at least twenty questions affirmatively, you probably *are* an introvert. This is neither positive nor negative. It is your preferred way of relating to people, places, and things. It's a style—a comfort level—not to be confused with shyness. Many people, including me, have equated introversion with shyness, but we've seen that shyness is a different personality type. Shyness contributes to anxiety and in its more severe state can even lead to major forms of depression.

Remember: introversion is *not* a negative personality trait. Given nurturing and perhaps some adjustments here and there to enhance our lifestyles, we introverts can be very fulfilled people. Introversion is a preference instead of an absolute need. But as noted before, introversion can become a barrier to success in many cases. So why not explore techniques to satisfactorily replace, disguise, or at least diminish introversion from the business side of your life, where extroverted qualities are typically noticed and rewarded?

In this book, the word *introversion* represents a chosen mode of behavior—which is neither depressed nor shy, although there are certainly instances where feelings of shyness overlap. However, keep in mind, that there are also shy extroverts.

What Types of People Are Extroverts, and What Types of People Are Introverts?

Extroverts go out to meet and greet the world and allow the world to come in and meet them. Extroverts are usually comfortable at parties, love to speak up at staff meetings, and like to converse on the phone. Extroverts can stand up before a group of people and expound on a topic they know practically nothing about. They can also talk themselves through a problem they need to solve: "Where is that report I was working on? I know I had it a minute ago. Let's see. I went into Jane's office to discuss the budget. . . . I know I had it in my hand in there—could not have contributed to the numbers without my copy. Then I went to get coffee; maybe I left it by the coffee pot. . . ." Extroverts talk in order to think. And with most extroverts, what you see is what you get.

Introverts are the people most driven to distraction by the spoken semi-internal dialogue extroverts are prone to conduct. Introverts don't like to outwardly complain. Instead, they roll their eyes and silently curse the darkness.

Extroverts are almost always comfortable in the world of superficial conversations and chatter. Visualize a staff meeting. The extroverted boss is sitting at the head of the table going around the room inquiring about how everyone's department is doing.

"So, John," she says. "How are things going with you this week?" "Great!" says John, your nemesis. "That new advertising line is right on target, and the numbers are looking really good. I should have the final concept nailed down by early next week!"

"And Gillian," says your boss, "what's up with marketing?" And Gillian, who you often feel would look better with an extremely sharp object protruding from her eye, says, "We are doing *so* well. We just landed the Jones account and are set to go to print next week. The T-shirts and balloons are in production. It's going to be a terrific campaign!"

"Oh barf," is what's going through your introverted brain. "This is *so boring*. We discussed this last week and John and Gillian said the same things. It's a good thing my boss can depend on me and my folks. We seem to be the only ones who are truly on some sort of a deadline here!"

And your boss finally comes around to you. "How's it going?" "Fine," you say, "everything is just fine." And it is. In your department, everything really is just fine. But guess what? Your boss does not know that, because you have not shared that with everyone. In fact, you have not shared that with anyone, and therefore no one knows that your department is actually doing better than John's and Gillian's put together.

You're working hard, things are going well, and you have neglected to share some of the most important information with the person or persons who may hold the key to your future in the organization. Why haven't you rung your own chimes?

Possibly because you feel that everyone really *does* know how well you're doing. But the truth is, they are so involved with their own business *they know nothing unless you tell them.* You need to let people know what is going on. How else are they going to know? By osmosis?

Extroverts are so busy tooting their horns that they can often suffer from "open mouth and insert foot" disease. Introverts are so busy doing what they are getting paid for, they often neglect to inform others of their success—with sometimes disastrous results! I coach extroverts to count to ten before they open their mouths. I coach introverts to remember to bring into meetings all the bells and whistles the extroverts carry unconsciously. Otherwise, your boss starts to think, "Hmmmm . . . I don't know what's wrong with Fredi. She just does not seem to fit into our culture here at the Sticky Widget Co. She appeared smart and eager when we hired her. Maybe she'd be happier somewhere else." See? This is turning into a disaster! Your introverted behavior has convinced your boss that you are not a team player—not a good position to be in when promotion time comes along.

The other real or perceived danger here is that because you have a tendency to keep thoughts and ideas to yourself, you may inadvertently neglect to share important information with your fellow team members. If they—and more importantly, your boss—later become blindsided by this news, you will have nailed your coffin shut. As redundant as it seems, and although you believe that everyone in the division knows what you are up to, trust me: they do not have a clue. You need to keep them in the loop again and again. This is *essential* for introverts.

As stated, extroverts love to go out into the world—and they love for the world to come to them. The United States certainly has a very extroverted culture. Look at our television programs, commercials, and movies, in which lots of people go to lots of parties, enjoy recreational activities (skiing, rollerblading), and dance, drink, and high-five each other at more parties and bars. All of this coming and going represents the American belief that in order to have the most fun, be the most successful, be the best looking, be with the best-looking people, have the smartest children, and have the best parties where all our friends have the best time, we must be "out there," highly energized, constantly interacting with our environment —all the time. This is not too helpful to introverts.

Introverts need to think first in order to talk. Introverts derive their energy from within. We are reflective and often need to "get back to people" rather than make instant decisions. With an introvert, what you see is what we allow you to see—because a lot of our thoughts, actions, and reactions are internalized.

The following chart provides a quick look at the different ways in which extroverts and introverts are energized, stimulated, and perceived. Some of the following characteristics are quite stereotypical.

Perceived Characteristics of Extroverts and Introverts

Extroverts	Introverts
Stimulated by the outside world of people, activities, and things	Stimulated by their internal world of ideas, emotions, and impressions
• Talkers	• Loners
• Externally oriented	• Internally oriented
• Blurt out thoughts without regard for others	• Withhold thoughts and opinions; withdrawn
• Interested in the breadth of things	• Interested in the depth of things
• Involved with people and things	• Non–team players
• Quick decision makers	• Contemplators of solutions
• Interactive	• Aloof or arrogant
• Prefer action and noise	• Prefer concentration and quiet
• Active brainstormers	• Independent workers
• Out-loud thinkers	• Reflective
• Do, think, do	• Think, do, think

For many years I have noticed my tendency, upon arriving home after a long day of training and interacting with clients, to proceed to find a million things to do in my apartment rather than relaxing and giving my body the rest it so desperately needs. Living solo, I find that a sense of relief washes over me when I close the door and I am finally *alone*. It's a subtle sensation (I now recognize), as my batteries begin to charge and I tell myself: "Now! Now! I can let the frolic begin. It's time to water the plants, add to that article I've been working on, play with the computer, take in just one more chapter in that mystery I'm reading, finish the newspaper, glance through another must-read magazine, or maybe even pay a bill"—all the while trying to remind myself that it is midnight and I have a 7:30 A.M. meeting the next day!

Is there a correlation between my desire to recharge myself and my introversion? Could be. Now that we've identified some of the introvert's personal energy sources, look at some of *your* unique personal lifestyle traits. And don't forget, as baseball giant Yogi Berra said, "You can learn a lot by watching"—especially when you observe yourself.

Interestingly, with the rapid rise of technology, a trend is quietly taking place. All of a sudden our very extroverted culture is starting to resemble introverted behavior.

In an interview conducted by Alex Chadwick on National Public Radio's *Morning Edition* program, Dr. Zimbardo commented on the effect this trend is having. He observed that children are growing up with fewer examples of natural daily interaction with strangers as technology replaces gas station attendants and bank tellers, as families get smaller, and computer games replace neighborhood games. He noted that, "we are losing the social lubrication that's essential for people to feel comfortable in the presence of each other," (August 30, 1995).

Extroverts need to beware! We introverts can thrive as systems planners and programmers, but the extroverts will find themselves becoming very bored and antsy in this introverted environment. All of us will need to find an antidote for a society that relies more and more on technology. Our society is also being forced into introversion by the chosen styles in which we live, as we pull away from the passé phenomenon known as "the community." Tom Halfhill, a *BYTE* senior news editor based in San Mateo, California, thinks that the rise of gated communities is unweaving the social fabric upon which this country was built. He believes that the evolution in the architecture of our homes reflects the shift from more extroverted actual communities to virtual communities that are introverted by their very nature. "The abrupt demise of the front porch isn't merely symbolic. It says a lot about how America has changed over the past fifty years and how new technology can significantly alter our communities and social relationships," (Halfhill 1994). Halfhill believes that if we continue the trend toward replacing our actual immediate communities with virtual extended communities, we will eventually find ourselves living in neighborhoods that will have become at best, "sterile and boring. At worst, they'll become hostile places where criminals fill the void of street life. Isolationism doesn't work any better locally than it does internationally, and the results can be equally self-destructive," (1994).

Our world is becoming more naturally introverted with the advent of virtual communities in which you interact more with your computer than with your boss. But this trend is not happening so rapidly that it means introverts can smugly retreat into their shells and wait for the world to adapt to their preferences. Networking remains an essential element in almost all business interactions. We introverts may like to think that the world Halfhill describes is the one in which we will finally fit in, one in which the extroverts will come to us for help; but the reality remains that networking, despite its reputation, is healthy both for your business and for the world. How can this be? you ask. Let's take a look at what "networking" really is.

(4)

Networking: A Matter of Asking for Information

"Ninety percent of this game is half mental."
YOGI BERRA

Networking is a concept that has been used, abused, overrated, and underrated. But when asked, most people cannot explain what it really is, with all its subtleties, or how it really works.

When we are faced with making a change—to a new job, a new city, or new neighborhood, new school, or any of the myriad other situations we experience—some of us panic. This book will help you overcome the fear of asking for information, which you especially need when making a life or situation change. Asking for information is basically what networking is all about! Asking people who may know more than you about a certain topic or person, and asking if they would be willing to share some of that knowledge, constitutes the art of successful networking. Yet for those of us who are shy, or are introverts, this simple concept can produce massive heart palpitations and major sweat.

Taking this one step further, let's look at networking as *the process of gathering information*. That's all. Nothing more. And if we called it Information Gathering 101, or market research, or just plain research, wouldn't you begin to breathe easier?

The job-search process offers a good example of information gathering.

We traditionally look for a job using a formal, linear method: reading the classifieds and answering ads, contacting a recruiter in our field, sending letters and resumes, and visiting our college alumni office. This process can be quite time-consuming and generally nets minimal results. We've all seen television news programs about the plight of laid-off workers, who send out over three hundred resumes and receive no response. They have not learned how to broaden their job-search skills or fully cultivated themselves for greater success—nor have they read this book.

A different technique—the one that sends shivers down the spines of those of us who consider ourselves introverts— is the informal search. The informal search, what we've come to know as networking, is a *lifelong process of building relationships with people*. Often these people help us to clarify and define our goals. They also can help us fine-tune our focus for a long and rewarding career. Once you determine the best information-gathering approach for *your* needs, you will effectively implement the networking technique.

Networking Through Life . . .

In today's business world, networking is critical for survival. There are five key reasons why you need to continually network. No matter how hard it may seem in the beginning to effectively network, the payoffs are so terrific that you may well decide the pain is worth the gain. But remember what I said earlier: *Why Should Extroverts Make All the Money?* is going to spare you the pain.

Because so many people are realizing the rewards of networking for jobs and careers, it is important to understand its history and its future impact. While studying at Harvard University three decades ago, Mark Granovetter wrote a doctoral dissertation titled *Changing Jobs—Channels of Mobility Information in a Suburban Population* (1970). He found that an astounding 75 percent of all jobs were secured through networking. Although this research was done some time ago, the statistics are still valid. But networking can make life easier in many other areas as well—in fact, sometimes it's impossible to get through the day without it. If you need a lawyer, a doctor, a baby-sitter, an academic tutor, or a neighborhood kid to mow your lawn, you'll have to network. Sure, you can try the Yellow Pages. But wouldn't you rather depend on referrals from friends and neighbors you trust, people who have already had good experiences with such service providers? Various networking connections and outcomes often go beyond simply finding a job. The act of connecting one person to another is what networking is all about. And today it's a way of living—even surviving. Because networking is so critical in our lives, let's explore some of the (often unexpected) ways to utilize networking—as well as confirm why it is so important to maintain our contacts.

Business/Social Connections

That we are connected to one another largely through the people we already know and the people that these people know emphasizes the fact that people are our greatest resource. The saying "I'll have my people call your people," suggests intentional networking—networking for a purpose. Often the purpose is to offer assistance, or to make arrangements. Networking is about helping one another. You help me, I'll help you; you initially arrange for the meeting, I'll make sure it happens; you refer a caterer, I'll locate the best space; help me secure the guest speaker, I'll contact the media and pull in the crowd; introduce me to the CEO or to your friend who knows the CEO, I'll return the favor someday.

So when a publisher of a food and wine magazine wanted to have a very high-profile chef contribute his expertise and name to his publication, he had to do some networking. He established an informal relationship with an industry consultant who knew the chef. As a first step, the publisher asked the consultant to initiate a letter of introduction on his behalf, and the connection was made. Reciprocities are not often specified, unless, as with almost all of the previous examples, the participants are currently engaged in a joint project that identifies their mutually beneficial roles. The point to remember is that we all know people who can help us or connect us to someone else. And, in return, we can, should, and will be of help to them, in some way, even if it's further down the road.

Uncovering Information We Can Use

During networking interactions, you will discover lots of things—information will become more available. In the job arena, through good networking conversations, you'll sometimes learn of planned company changes and new opportunities, current and future trends in your industry, ad or publicity campaigns about to unfold, or the names of important people you should know.

When starting a new job, going to a new city on a business trip, or taking a vacation, for example, information is vital. I have coached many clients about to derail from super careers simply because they did not gather important information—not data information but *people* information—they needed in their new environments. Which person in this division has the most power? (Sometimes it is not the name on the top of the official organizational chart.) Who is the secretary—the person you need to befriend in order to improve your work flow? Who is the administrative assistant? Who knows the most about the company?

Getting a jump on the information is one way to put yourself in the lead in any job competition. Even though you can discover many things through other sources, networking usually offers the most current information. Which organizations are getting married? Divorced? Sleeping together without a commitment? By networking you can get the "skinny"—learn the gossip before the news hits the street. Networking also keeps your name in people's minds—or in someone's Rolodex—to fill a chair that no one else knows has been vacated. In other words, networking gives you exposure and visibility.

Greater Exposure

Let's say you really want to become a professional photographer. Are you going to keep your photographs hidden in your studio drawer? Of course not. Introverts can comfortably expose themselves, too—to the everyday cameras of life. By simply talking about mutually interesting topics with others, visibility will automatically result. Attending activities inside and outside your business environment enables others to think of you or remember you when a desirable situation arises. We don't only want to discover information, we also want to *be* discovered—be promoted or hired or commissioned for that special project. But we have to let others know about us.

I have found that many introverts are so confident that someone is going to recognize their greatness that they don't even try to increase their exposure. This reminds me of a story a man from Japan shared with me. He was taught to be deferential and to do his work, and for that, he would be rewarded. After receiving his M.B.A., he went to work for a major American bank. At the start of every year, someone would be selected by his boss to go for credit training. My client really wanted this training—he needed it in order to fulfill his career profile. After years of watching coworkers who were sent for training receive promotions, he finally became courageous and angry enough to ask his boss why he had not been chosen. Certainly it was not any flaw in his work. His boss looked at him in astonishment and said, "But you never asked! I didn't know you wanted to go!"

This reflects what my grandfather, who was from Barbados, constantly repeated: "If you don't ask, you don't get!" He was full of these simple little sayings that to this day continue to be both true and precious to me.

Learning More About Ourselves

Learning more about yourself enables you to discover or affirm what you want, what you are willing to do, and what you are best suited for. In her earlier working life, Marsha (my writing partner for this book, who, as mentioned in the introduction, is mainly an extrovert, but has significant degrees of introversion), worked in New York City universities. A college counselor, she often had lunch with fellow counselors from another department. Her original goal was to apply her counseling experience and interest toward this other department as soon as the opportunity presented itself. Through these lunches and growing friendships, Marsha began to learn more about her colleagues' jobs. She learned that the other counselors had to specialize in and teach academic subjects to large rotating groups of students enrolled in the program—in addition to spending lots of time updating lesson plans and other more tedious tasks. In her existing position, she had more freedom to directly influence her students, and Marsha realized she didn't want to sacrifice this comfortable one-on-one student-counseling relationship. Later, when she gave up the counseling job to manage her department's program, Marsha learned still more about herself: she preferred sitting in her neat, attractive, and quiet office writing project proposals and describing the program's overall creative vision much more than the department politics and directing the staff and all the intricate and very challenging day-to-day activities. She had enjoyed taking charge while interacting with her students, but there was a limit to how far she wanted to go. She could have done without the extra headaches that came with the territory.

So life is about experimenting and learning. At times you can obtain important information before you become involved in something that may not be a good or great fit. The more you talk to others—or network—the more you will learn. The exercises in this book will also help you to learn more about who you really are. How can you tell other people what you want to do if you don't know yourself?

Nurturing Our Passions

Finding and realizing our passion helps us to successfully target and propel us toward a career that suits us. And nurturing our passions improves our quality of life.

Have you noticed that even introverts who are discussing subjects about which they're passionate seem to just unleash and "let it flow"? Yes, introverts, too, go nuts when communicating their passions. When we truly feel passionate about something (or someone), it's easy to express it. Richard Bolles, the famed author of *What Color Is Your Parachute?*, writes, "shyness yields in the face of love." In these instances we freely share our thoughts, creative ideas, and knowledge. Many of the people that I interviewed demonstrated such positive expressiveness once they identified or discovered their great passion.

Try incorporating your passions in networking exercises. Make it a point to verbally express yourself about your passionate interests to experience the ease in which you *can* communicate and participate in a business or social situation. The practice will help you get in the habit of talking and seeking information from others. I can talk forever about my passions—such as my love of sports. Later, I will share my self-discovery ideas and how I make my passions work for me. Try this "talking around your passions" exercise first around your friends and then at your next business or social event. It works, once you open up to it.

One of the first times I realized the importance of "passion" was a few years ago as I was working with a client who was about to be downsized. Barbara was a successful vice president at a major New York City banking institution known for its cutting-edge technology. Her division had done all of the innovation and design for the early automated teller machines. Working with programmers, she and her team had designed the user-friendly screens that make our lives easy when we need cash on the weekends. Unfortunately, her division was eliminated when their work was completed—long before "ATM" became part of our vocabulary. Barbara was frightened but ready to get on with her life. She thought staying with the bank was a viable option; however, in order to accertain what was happening in the rest of the institution, she needed to do some networking. But she could not do it. Barbara found it physically impossible to pick up the phone and ask others for information.

The Myers-Briggs Type Indicator (MBTI) was not the only instrument we used in the early phases of the assessment process. We also looked at her strengths, interests, transferable skills, and knowledge. Because Barbara was having such a difficult time with the networking process, I decided to review all of her assessments and highlight those things in which she expressed an interest. Nowhere did she indicate interest in anything related to the banking industry.

She had been lucky and successful in her last position, but her job really had nothing to do with banking. It involved designing a product that people would feel comfortable using. In reality, although Barbara had worked in "electronic banking," a growing and important field in the mid-1980s, Barbara did not care about banking or the financial-services industry at all!

What *was* Barbara passionate about? Her two main interests were politics and women's issues. The hard work was making Barbara realize that her transferable skills (problem solving, strategic planning, budgeting) could go with her anywhere, to any industry!

Barbara began to reposition herself. She was able to see that banking was not for her, and began to take baby steps outside—speaking with people who were working in organizations associated with women and politics. What a surprise! The networking became easier because she was now discussing things she cared about. It became much easier to ask for information. She began by saying, "I have a background in banking, but my job actually focused on making people feel comfortable about technology. Let me share some of our challenges at the bank and tell you how we solved the problems. I'd like to know whether you think I can apply my experience in the not-for-profit arena."

Because Barbara was comfortable and passionate about the information she was seeking, she began to enjoy the networking process. Yes, it took time for Barbara to wade into unfamiliar territory. However, once she began the process, it grew easier all the time. Doors began opening for her, and she found herself in industries that she never dreamed she would be a part of. The combination of politics and women's issues landed her a position in an internationally recognized organization that deals with women and reproductive health!

5

CASE STUDIES: UP CLOSE AND PERSONAL

"You got to be careful if you don't know where you're going, because you might not get there."

YOGI BERRA

Writing *Why Should Extroverts Make All the Money?* has allowed me to reflect on the many individuals—introverted and extroverted—that I meet through my business (one-on-one career-management coaching and "Networking for Introverts" seminars). In this chapter, I've included many of my clients' insightful and compelling personal experiences, recounted during my interviews (their names are changed to protect their privacy). They highlight the day-to-day encounters we all experience, and show how we can all improve many aspects of our careers—and our lives. As I continued to interview one introvert after another, I was struck by the common patterns—shared experiences, emotions, and settings—among each person's areas of growth.

Unlike readers of this book, I had the pleasure and benefit of face-to-face interaction with my clients. And although the words and feelings they expressed were serious, and I knew that many of my clients had experienced various degrees of pain, I was delightfully struck by their sense of humor. As I spoke to my fellow introverts, we shared the ability to laugh at ourselves and our difficulties in doing things that appeared so easy for others. I should mention, however, that not all of these stories reflect 100 percent success.

Realizing Introversion

Portia is an introvert who heads the volunteer division of a not-for-profit organization working with mentors for children. She had resigned as CEO of a women's philanthropic not-for-profit organization when it relocated to Washington; she and I worked together on her transition.

During our conversation, Portia explained that she had assumed leadership positions that she probably would have avoided had she been a more obvious introvert. She believes a number of forces persuaded her to accept leadership roles in her work. But when we worked together and discussed the fact that she is an introvert, Portia grew more comfortable with the prospect of something other than a top leadership role. "I became much more aware of the fact that it fit my nature not to be the most public person around," she said. This does not mean introverts cannot function in leadership roles. It does mean, however, that introverts in leadership positions should be aware of and comfortable in their introversion.

In the workplace, Portia tends to resist organized social activities. "I do like to have impromptu intellectual conversations in the office," she said, and she attends and contributes to meetings—but she shies away from the social after-work stuff. At an off-site function, however, Portia attempted to overcome her inclinations by sharing a room with a colleague. "I really tried to fall into that collective spirit, because that was part of the value system of the organization," Portia told me.

Portia found that she could unwind from the exhausting meetings by watching TV—but her roommate hated television. Not only that, her roommate always wanted to discuss everything that had taken place in the meeting they had just attended. Portia needed her own room just so she could take control of the environment and turn on the TV and listen to voices, without having to take part in conversations herself. But Portia treated her desire for her own room as not legitimate—but it really was.

"It was very important to me," she said.

> I found that if I didn't do this, I would not be able to function at all. Therefore, in the interest of being able to function, I had the right to carve out space for myself—to be alone. That was an important piece of self-knowledge for me. That it's not only OK, but that it's *essential* that I have time alone, to be able to function publicly. And, going further, I now know that I need to build in "alone time," both before and after meetings, and similar types of events, especially if I know I'm going to have an intense time being with people. I don't think of it anymore as being strange and something I should fight against. Now I see that this is just the way I am. Giving myself permission to say "no" to something is important. I think the thing I'm struggling with now is that I can choose too much isolation, perhaps more than what is good for me. I have experienced times where I can now spend time with people and feel elated by it and think, "Oh this does not feel so bad." But still only small groups. It's easy for me to do too much, and I know when it's too much because I get cranky.

Having moved on, today Portia has a fund-raising position that, naturally, requires her to network all the time. It seemed like a good job, but we both knew it would be a stretch. She says it still feels very difficult for her, and it's still frustrating. She finds that she is asking for more help from her board of directors, in terms of facilitating and setting up contacts—which she finds very difficult and may convince her to walk away from this job. She hasn't been very successful in raising money, and she believes that fund-raising is much like sales. And looking at successful sales techniques, Portia sees the process as very different from who and what she is. She realizes that she has to stay motivated about the goals, and some times are easier than others. And there is a difference between doing it for herself and doing it for a cause, she explained.

> I wrote a position paper and had a conversation with a board member about it. She told me she didn't get the feeling that I was passionate about my position. I think that I have passionate feelings about issues, and this was an issue I cared about deeply. But I think that as an introvert, I am not likely to demonstrate my passion in a way that is very flashy or public. I have internal feelings about issues, and whether they are issues I'm fund-raising for or networking on my own behalf for, it is not my nature to be enthusiastic or external. I approach them because I've decided they are important, and I wouldn't be doing it if I thought otherwise. But to people who are looking for something more, I think they get a sense of detachment from me, and from the issue. I will intellectualize it, which is very Waspy. Introverts process everything internally. It's "internal intensity." So when I talk about race and gender, for example, I can go on and on. But I may

be continuing the conversation internally, away from others.

Portia was taking a writing course, and her class was discussing *Paradise* by Toni Morrison. In one scene, Portia related, Morrison describes one of the women saying that she had never met a man who didn't come across as an "unlit firecracker." But, Portia lamented, "Why am I even bothering to write? I could never write a phrase like that." She had argued with her instructor for a couple of days on this point—but it was an internal argument. She believes that she is keeping herself in check—she argues with herself while driving to the office in the morning, rather than becoming argumentative in class—because she doesn't want to disrupt the class with her own introverted fears.

Portia also views managing introverts, including her assistant, Stacey (whom we will meet later), as an internal process.

> I wanted a support person who would anticipate what I needed and not make me have to articulate to her why or where or when things had to be done. I said to my administrative assistant, "I want you to manage me." And as she got into the job, she, as an introvert, was able to do that. She was a detailed person and could anticipate levels of the job that I did not want to be bothered with. I did need a mind reader. And when I didn't get those kinds of people, I thought of them as incompetent—was very quick to judge them and was very harsh in my judgment. When I think back, it was simply that they were people who needed a lot of external direction, more than I was willing, or knew how, to give or wanted to be bothered giving, or wanted to think about.

And Portia's mother, and other people who know her, agree that she does need someone who will anticipate things, someone who can partner with a visionary.

Accepting Introversion

Carolyn is a sole-practitioner attorney who has always hit a wall when working in a large corporate setting. She came to me after leaving several large firms whose cultures were not suited to her personality. She is now happy working for herself. Carolyn fought being classified as an introvert, because she was raised to think that there was something very wrong with people who were shy or introverted. She was told not to behave that way, so she has spent her life compensating. This inability to be comfortable in her own skin has gotten her into trouble on several occasions. She loves quiet and solitude, but feels guilty for this desire. Carolyn also feels she should be "on" all the time.

As in most of these interviews, I started out by asking her, "As an introvert, have you been aware of your introversion and have you felt different from others?"

Not hesitating, Carolyn responded calmly, focused and determined, and her answer (unlike the answers from most of the others, when asked this question) surprised me:

"I was never aware of my introversion; I was a talkative child. I would take center stage and be told to keep quiet. I knew I had to go through these acts, which is why I always called it performing. I just assumed that everybody put on an act. I didn't feel it was unnatural."

"Did I catch you in a 'performance' today?" I asked her.

"I guess so," she responded, "because as I've said, I've been performing all of my life, and I'm exhausted from it. It really never occurred to me that everyone was not putting on an act. I never actually thought about it. Can you imagine growing up always being aware of putting on an act? This is how I was trained."

I was shocked that Carolyn considered herself as having been "trained" instead of "raised." I wanted her to tell me more about what that was like. She shared with me that when she was a child, her mother would just say, "talk!" "As if it were that easy," Carolyn said.

"Open up your mouth! You don't have any right to be silent," my mother would command. She may have viewed my silence as me being judgmental of others. I think that's why I read so much. When I opened up a book, she'd leave me alone. I think she thought, "Ah, what a smart and wonderful child, reading, while everyone else watches television." As long as I read she left me alone.

Carolyn now realizes that introversion was always her salvation. That's where she would go for peace—to get closer to who she was. She told me she also loved to be around older people. "But whenever I want to get out and go crazy with other people, I can do that as well," she interjected.

Politics and working with politicians became one of her comfortable career choices. I was again a little surprised, until she explained that with a career in politics, she could sit in a corner and do her work, while the politicians themselves were (and needed to be) out there glad-handing the public:

They needed that, but *I* didn't have to be the one out in front, doing the speeches. *I* could even get a car and a loudspeaker and go around the neighborhood telling people to get out and vote. But that was protected. It was in the car and it was literally

campaigning for someone else. My own networking is much more difficult.

Part of my problem is that I've never learned to
articulate things that could be done for me. It gets
in my way with marketing the business. I can market my services to others, but not to my friends. I
have difficulty with people I know, because I feel
I'm a burden. I don't want to be part of an IOU. I
just want to go in clean, knowing that I don't owe
anyone anything. For instance, when I am doing a
real estate deal, I can be a bitch on wheels. However, if I am doing the deal with or for someone I
know, or have some kind of relationship with, the
deal then becomes a lot more difficult. I would need
to rehearse and coach myself into doing what I have
to do to see the transaction through to the end.

With a stranger, in the middle of any negotiation, Carolyn
can really be tough, because "it's professional." She added,
"We are there to get the job done, and we accomplish that.
When I am working with someone I know, personally, it's very
difficult and sometimes they might perceive me to be a real
pushover. But I'm not, when I'm in business—only when I
think I have to ask people I know for a favor."

I asked Carolyn how she acted in business meetings. And
was she comfortable going to functions after work or joining
her colleagues for a drink on Fridays?

I'm very comfortable in meetings, but I am always
prepared. In fact, I *over*prepare. Otherwise there
would be a nervousness when it comes to speaking,
and I thought of taking Toastmasters to help with
that. But I'm a researcher, so once I do my home-

work, I'm then very comfortable in meetings—well, kind of . . . because I really do prepare. I could never talk off the top of my head.

With work social functions, it depends. I've learned over the years to get more comfortable with this. I used to be really uncomfortable, but I've taught myself that I need to make a conscious decision to do it, and it certainly is essential when it comes to building my business. So I ask myself: Should I be with this group? Is this professional? Do I have something else I'd rather be doing than being with these people? I am picky and choosy in terms of who I want to be with. I can go have a drink with one friend. But sometimes I feel I'd rather be home in the bed reading a book or getting a real old movie. Sometimes I think introverts are just weird!

I asked Carolyn whether she believed, in her heart of hearts, that being an introvert had held her back in certain ways in her career. "Absolutely," was her quick response.

I always feel that I must come in with a defined objective. To me, introversion is a dangerous trait. It gives me a lot of face validity, but I don't reach out when I need to reach out. Meanwhile, the extroverts are out there shmoozin' and boozin'. And I don't even have a mentor to help [me]. Of course I would do it for someone else [mentor], but I can't stand it when someone does it for me.

And I hate the parties, especially the Christmas parties. All the sucking up, the gifts, the lunches, all of that is agonizing. For me, all of that is a stretch. It's draining. But since I know I have to do it, I realize it was easier when I worked for somebody else rather than to have to do all of that stuff myself. But, now that I am working for myself, it's great to have a partner, especially one who is the opposite of me. So, when it comes to much of the social affairs, I tell myself "my partner can do it."

"But we all could use help at some point to better manage our careers," I reminded her. "When I proposed networking to help you, what was your first thought?"

Again, I thought, I don't want to burden my friends. I had been working in this profession for twelve years. The last time I was downsized, before I started my own firm, I felt that networking was going to make me feel like a failure. I did not want my friends to know that I was looking for a job again. I took it personally and was especially concerned about how I was being perceived. My sister, the extrovert, would view it as "who cares . . . as long as I get what I want." But she wasn't walking in my shoes. And I obviously don't see things her way. It was very personal for me. I like people, but I don't want to be a burden to anyone. *I* want to be the one who can help people. I don't want anyone helping me; I can do it myself. Then I don't owe anybody anything and I'm not a burden. And I don't want to think about: What will somebody think of me? I know they're not going to reach out to help like I would reach out to help.

And though I network all of the time now for my business, it will never be comfortable. But I have to do it. It's painful! I apologize all over the place. "Oh thank you so much for talking to me. . . ." Oh my God! I'm a lawyer, for God's sake, and I feel as if I owe these people my life! But I love the art of making the deal, like Donald Trump. I like the transactional stuff. Taking the "dot" and expanding it into a something. Development and community development. Making sure the deal closes. I love the politics of it. I love creating the written documents. Negotiations. The research. The number crunching. Teaching. I love working with municipalities and getting them to buy into the deal. I would love to be in entertainment law as well. I just don't like the networking part.

Considering her last position at the car-rental firm, I wondered whether Carolyn believed her introverted "differences" contributed to her reasons for leaving.

"I think so. I could not control the extroverted, somewhat 'out of control' side of me," she said. Now Carolyn sees that instead of quietly trying to figure out the politics of the organization, she was intent on being a "know-it-all." When she left her previous job at a not-for-profit organization, before joining the car-rental company, she was on a high! She had been working with brilliant consultants. And no one could tell her anything, she admitted.

I had been spoiled and coddled. I came into the car-rental business without a mid-ground attitude. My attitude was "You take me or you don't." My problem in that company was my personality, with those managers and the general counsel who I reported to. With my independence, I thought I knew it all, and they could not tell me anything. I missed the obvious fact that a car-rental company is a manufacturing, blue-collar environment. I didn't get a handle on the culture. I have since learned, through you, that "It's my job to make my boss look good." I never learned to take direction. I was not humble. I didn't listen. I saw myself in an attorney role and I started to perform, like when I was a child. I didn't listen. Everyone told me I was shooting myself in the foot, but no one told me to shut up and listen! No one told me to stop. No one told me: "Carolyn, this is the way things go. They're in charge, you're not, and you are going to have to find a way to work with them. Period." Unfortunately, I didn't consider executive coaching until after that.

Carolyn, at that point, was caught in the classic "introvert trying to behave like an extrovert" syndrome. Instead of being quiet, thoughtful, and reflective—her natural self—she tried to become more and more dominant. She was not thinking clearly. And it blew up in her face.

At her next firm, Carolyn thought she had learned her lesson. She just kept saying, "Oh yes, I can do that. I can do that"—whatever they wanted. And she never reached out for help. In fact, she was ashamed to ask questions, like: What are your expectations? How are you going to train me? How much time will I have for this training?

The problem was, I had answers but was clueless about the questions. I didn't ask those questions because I wasn't feeling worthy of more. I felt that that was all I could get. "If these folks are going to pay me $150,000 per year, I better have all of the answers," I thought. So I never asked the questions.

And I never got the answers, or at least sufficient information. This affected my interaction with my bosses. I was so busy doing it all by myself. Although my boss was a creep. He was one of those people they just kept around because it was easier than getting rid of him. Everyone knew how to manage my boss except me. There were a lot of shady deals going on there.

You know, some people make choices at the drop of a hat. Then there are those of us who take fifty hours to make sure we're doing the right thing. A friend of mine often said, "Stop thinking about it and just do it." So I guess introversion can not only impact our ability to perform our jobs, but it can also impact our credibility.

Finally, I asked Carolyn how she thought her introversion affected her interaction with her family, friends, and personal or business partners today.

I have no idea. I'm outspoken with them. I am very empathetic to their pain, but I don't think they are empathetic to mine. They see me as the strong person that they can dump everything on. But I'm not. That's just what I portray. I really need to know that there are others out there who are experiencing what I've experienced and that although I now feel successful, I am not alone.

Learning the Safety of Introversion

Stacey has a B.A. degree and a history of underemployment. She is currently an assistant program manager in a major not-for-profit organization. Stacey worked for Portia, whom we met earlier, as her administrative assistant.

Unlike Carolyn, Stacey was aware of her introversion early on in her life, especially when it came to certain situations. "I'm not comfortable when I feel I don't know a lot or when I'm not exactly sure about what I know. Although I feel I know myself, I still may accept a negative comment," Stacey explained. In her job (a foundation that focuses on women's issues), the program administrators often pressure Stacey's department to reach out to more grassroots organizations, such as affiliations within the arts, to expand their programs. At times Stacey had ideas about how to make that happen— but when she's sitting around the table with other people whom she deems to know more than she does, and *they* are not speaking up, she won't speak up either. Though she knows there are other things they could be doing for the program, she doesn't feel that she's in a position to speak out. "And even though I've been invited to the meeting and am a part of the staff, I feel I have 'no right' to express an opinion on the improvement of the program," she said.

Like Carolyn, Stacey was encouraged—or challenged— to speak up when she was growing up.

"When I was growing up, I was encouraged to share my opinions," she said. "I lived with my great-aunt, who is very extroverted. In fact, she's quite the social butterfly. Everybody knows her; she's the schoolteacher, and all her students love her. Everybody loves her. She always said, 'Don't be shy. Go up there and read your piece for Sunday School.' "

When Stacey was an adolescent, she moved back to New York with her mom, who is very introverted.

> My mother wanted me to be extroverted. She wanted me to go out there and experience the world and do all these fabulous things that she couldn't

do comfortably herself. I just felt like . . . Gee! Maybe I'm supposed to do all of these extroverted things, like my aunt, so I would try. I faked it. I did talent shows, but I never did individual pieces. I only did group performances. When we had dance performances, I only danced within the group and I would always put myself way off to the side or in the back. I never wanted to be in the front. I didn't like individual attention. I remember in high school, I received one honor, for English, and I worked up a sweat going up to the stage to shake the principal's hand.

But then there were moments when Stacey remembers clearly wanting to be an extrovert. She told me that she just didn't want to be different.

I didn't want to be the kid in the corner that no one recognized. So when I was getting ready to go to the high school prom, as usual I didn't have a date. And I didn't want to have to go with my cousin Darryl again. He always filled in, because I *never* had a date. So I decided that I was going to have a date! I was going to go and find myself a date, a *real* date. My mom didn't believe me. "How is this child ever going to find a date? She never had one before," I could hear her think.

But when introverts are determined to do something, it's amazing what they can accomplish. So "shy" Stacey went out, found a guy, spoke to him, and . . . voilà! Stacey had a date for her prom.

"I refused to be that different," Stacey asserted. "I got pushed to the point where I really didn't want to be that different from everybody else. My introversion was making me angry."

Does Stacey feel comfortable going out, today, with her coworkers? No, but she pushes herself to participate socially at functions during and after work.

> When I have gone out for a drink or to other functions, I'm comfortable in my little clique, but not with the people above me. I'm comfortable only with people on my level—my peers. But my boss is very extroverted, and she tries to force her extroversion on me, and that's very, very uncomfortable.

Because Stacey sticks to what she knows and what makes her feel comfortable and safe, she admits that in this way her introversion has interfered with her career advancement. For example, she's uncomfortable about asking for more money, yet she feels she deserves to earn more. "I'm uncomfortable, even with a lot of prompting from the people around me telling me to go for a better position. *They* think I'm qualified, now *I* just need to believe it. There's a position I know I'm qualified for, and I'm not going for it. It's just very, very difficult. . . . And, you know, I *hate* looking for a job."

As Stacey's coach, I've encouraged her to stay at her new job for a while and get some not-for-profit program experience under her belt before looking for another position, but the reality is that she could stay in this position forever and never take a risk. She could be reasonably comfortable and never receive any mentoring or learn new skills. But would she really want to do that?

In order for me to leave a job, I have to be so uncomfortable that I can't stand it anymore. I stayed at the bank for five years before they eliminated my position. Yet I hated numbers, I hated banking, I hated my job. I wasn't exceptionally good at it either, but I stayed, because it was not yet extremely uncomfortable. I mean, it was more comfortable than the alternative—which is to go out and look for a job. I hate going on interviews where people I don't know ask me to tell them about myself. I just hate that.

Stacey told me she came to me for coaching when she was about to "lose her mind" in her working environment. "And practicalities and common sense will always prevail, because I just can't afford to quit a job if I don't have another job. Financially that's impossible." Stacey went on to say that she's been fortunate enough, though, to fall into jobs where the people around her have encouraged and nurtured her. She's never been in a position where she has not been encouraged to aim higher. And that's a blessing in itself.

But Stacey has a very low tolerance for "nonintelligent" questions from people *she* gives direction to. I explained that, in some situations, Stacey's low tolerance for questions from others partly contributes to her not asking questions herself. She thinks asking questions is stupid, so she becomes her own worst enemy. This offers another explanation for why, in most staff meetings, she doesn't ask for or receive better direction and clarification. This, perhaps unintentional, arrogance *and* her introversion chokes her.

Stacey agrees.

Definitely, and I have been trying to step outside of my introversion. I've watched myself grow in the past six months by huge leaps and bounds. One of the times was during my most recent job search. It took me so long to pick up the phone and call Marcia (who is now my boss). Everyone told me she would be a good networking contact. It was just to find out information. It took much prodding and finally treating the phone call as a homework assignment; what was the worst thing that could happen? What caused me to grow was to step outside of my introversion and just make the call. Nothing really bad happened. In fact, I got a new job. I had always gone to agencies to do temp work instead of looking for a "real" job. Now I have a job with more money, and I really like the work that I do, though I do want it to be more sports related. But I've made a couple of contacts, and I practice networking techniques. This is not exactly my ideal job, but it's on the way.

In fact, Stacey subsequently had a conversation with a cousin and a woman connected with the Women's National Basketball Association (WNBA). Her cousin asked her the same question I asked: "What is your dream job?" And the woman from the WNBA told Stacey that if she really wanted to follow her sports-inclined dream job, she could introduce her to someone at the WNBA, Nike, and the AFL. She told Stacey that she could arrange for each of them to see her. But, Stacey had to follow up with phone calls. I had already taught her, of course, that if you don't follow up with your networking, you can't expect others to help you in the future. So Stacey made the phone calls. According to Stacey, "I've learned that it's easier for me to call if I know I'm going to get voicemail. And happily, people do answer their voicemails." And as a result, she met someone for lunch and made a connection at the Woman's Sports Foundation. Staccy maintained the contact. And her connections are actually starting to lead her toward her dream.

I later asked Stacey how valuable the Myers-Briggs Type Indicator was during her job search. Did taking the personality test help her clarify past promotions and career success?

> Yes, it clarified some career walls for me. It reinforced some of the things that I knew and gave me a very clear picture of myself. It reinforced my values. Finally after all these years of my family pushing me out there, there it was. There was a feeling of relief and that everything was OK. I feel 50 percent of my family is really introverted, and the only time they're not is when they are doing what they do best—preaching and teaching. That's their passion.
>
> As for me, I called myself a nerd, and sure enough I found out—I really am a nerd. And I am really comfortable with that. My husband calls me that all the time. I have attracted nothing but nerds, when it comes to men, including my introverted husband. We are two nerds together, and we do nerdy things. We walk our two dogs, we play on our computers, and we sing in the church choir. But, my introversion still affects my interactions with other members of my family and my friends. It generally stops me from saying what's really on my mind. The question remains: "Who am I?" Every time I think I'm talking about myself, I'm describing someone else, like my husband. I try to go away and come back with an intelligent thought, but, again, I am my own worst enemy. I know that I have an opinion, but it's easier for me to write a

paper on my perspective. I can definitely put my theories and thoughts down on paper.

I know I have to speak sometimes though. After all, people can't write down the things they want to say all the time! This is an area where my work concerning my introversion has paid off. If we have five meetings at work, for example, I'll speak out at maybe two—but before, I wouldn't speak out at all. My boss is also the kind of person who encourages speaking out, and I will, but I don't like her to feed me lines. If I'm going to speak, I will use my own voice. I've spoken to her about this and it's gotten a lot better.

I commended Stacey for approaching her boss. She agreed but pointed out that

everything is a process. When I called Portia, my old boss, that also was a very difficult thing to do, even though we worked together for two years. And although it was about work-related things, it was still hard. I needed to ask her some questions and I didn't want her to think I was just using her to get ahead—to my next place.

"But Stacey, isn't that what business is all about?" I quickly interjected.

Sure, you're right, but it's still very, very difficult for me. In fact, thinking back, when you originally proposed networking to help me with my career and job search, my first thought was, Is she *crazy*?

She wants me to talk to strangers, talk to people I don't know? How do you do that? I still have problems with it. And I see other people, and they do it, and they do it with such flair, and I feel as if I'm stumbling around like a jerk. Like when someone suggested I call so-and-so's sister. I start thinking— why do I need to call her? I don't need to call her. What could she possibly do for me? I get chills; I get a stomachache. I get really scared, really uncomfortable. Just the thought of it . . . .

And at a conference in Chicago, my old boss gave me the names of three people I could talk to while I was there. The conference lasted four days. It took me *two days* to contact these people. And I really only connected with one of them. Even talking about networking *now* gives me a headache.

It's not always easy to make connections—especially connections that will have lasting meaning. But when Stacey called me a month ago for some coaching, she left her name on my voicemail, adding that she wasn't sure I would remember her. But, I did her outplacement. We worked together for several months—just six months earlier!

I asked Stacey how she thinks her introversion impacts her ability to perform her job, as well as her credibility and her ability to manage others.

There are parts of my job that involve me calling our grantees. Some of them I know, so that's not too bad. But it's hard calling the ones I don't know, even the ones I *have* connected with. It's hard for me to separate the fact that I'm not calling for myself, but I'm calling on behalf of the foundation.

My boss wants us to connect with the world. So she wants me to do cold calling. Cold calling is horrendous! It's the worst thing next to the bubonic plague. I cannot comprehend how salespeople sit all day long and do cold calling—talking to perfect strangers. How many people want to do that? Right now I have to call a magazine and find out where I can find the woman who wrote a particular article, to then track down the recipients of some grant money. I have put off this call for as long as possible. I needed to do it yesterday!

But contrary to that, and to my amazement, just this week I did some cold calling and networking. I had lunch with someone who knows people from the NBA. It was a lot of sports-industry networking. I made one call to a woman who I knew was out of town, which was cool because I wanted to have my questions more together, so I left her a voice message. You see, as I keep saying, this is still anxiety-producing for me, I'm still very uncomfortable in the process, but I do it because there are goals to be met. And it works. I know it does. There's gold at the end of the rainbow, I just have to keep moving the process along. As painful as it is, I try to put that aside to achieve what I need to achieve. I now realize that this is the only way. And it's getting better, but I'm never going to love it.

Excommunication or Introversion?

Cecilia is a singer-songwriter and leader of her own band from England. Working in strategic positioning and marketing for a cutting-edge HMO by day, she feels somewhat "stuck" at her managed health plan company. She is conscious of her introversion, and she too feels that she is different from others. Cecilia feels that her introversion has prevented her from really pursuing her chosen musical career.

"I've been aware of being introverted and not being as comfortable around people. I feel I'm not one of the team, and I feel more isolated because of it," she explained.

Cecilia likes doing her own thing, but she feels that people do ignore her; they bypass her, go around her, and they don't include her. They think she's not interested in whatever they are interested in.

As a child, Cecilia didn't think she was very introverted. However, she played the piano, which is a fairly solitary thing to do. And she played with her Lego set, which is also a fairly solitary activity and one that requires imagination.

> When I played, I would have imaginary dialogues. And I never was into team sports because I had dislocated my kneecaps when I was very young and that prevented me from doing a lot of things. So, I wasn't on the hockey team or the net-ball team. I ended up swimming, which again is a fairly solitary sport. I only noticed becoming solitary when I was about thirteen or fourteen, though. At that time, I was smoking cigarettes in the bathrooms with all of the other girls who were smoking. But all the girls who were smoking were not really like me, and all the girls who were like me weren't smoking. By "like me" I mean middle-class. I hung out with sort of lower-class girls who were smoking and sleeping around. I just hung out with them in school. I didn't sleep around. But it served again to isolate me and not be "chatty Cathy" with the

middle-class girls. Then I started dating people that were a lot older than me. So that also separated me.

In class though, Cecilia related, she was not the quiet person in the back. She went on to say that in certain situations she can be quite a verbal person.

I think that's the flip-flop side of me. If everyone else in the room is an introvert, you can be damned sure I am going to speak up. And I was always the one who painted the lewd pictures that were too bad to put up on the walls. I think that people felt that that was an extroverted statement, but it really wasn't. I was just pushing the envelope.

Today, in the workplace, Cecilia tends to take a long time before she speaks. And when she does speak, she often isn't heard.

I feel as if I must squeak "excuse me" over and over before I'm noticed. The person next to me will be pushing and shoving in order to get their point heard, and I always feel their point is really not that important. Rather than battle, if someone does not say "Cecilia, do you have something to say?" I'll just sit there quietly. But in a meeting, if no one is taking any control, I will then slip into an extroverted role to try to bring some purpose to our being there. I'll say something like, "OK, what's going on?" to try to push it along.

> At my job, I have found that marketing is per-
> ceived as an extroverted function. But I perceive
> marketing to be a more introverted function. The
> majority of my work is done at my desk doing
> research over the phone or via E-mail. Maybe 25
> percent of my time is spent in meetings, which I
> really don't like. And most of my meetings are spent
> with people who are more senior than I am (like
> medical directors).

Cecilia said she doesn't manage "up" very well either. "I
carry all those old-fashioned values into meetings, like 'You're
older and I'm young, and so therefore I probably don't know
what I'm talking about.' Just out of respect, I feel I am supposed to think they know more than I do."

And when it comes to going out for the after-work drink,
she said she fails, because like so many introverts and shy
people, she hates these functions. Many introverted and
shy people find it awkward, so they generally just don't do it.
Cecilia stated that she would rather spend her time with one of
her other friends. And she also doesn't like being in groups,
which did not surprise me. "I am much better one-on-one.
Often my attention gets so diffused when everyone is talking
in groups. I can't concentrate, so I go off into my own world.
Even in my social life, I tend to see people one-on-one as well.
I find it's just more productive, and I know I deal better on
that level."

But Cecilia accepts her introversion only up to a point—
and then she begins to feel terribly left out. Like when her
job has off-site meetings:

> Everyone is supposed to be sharing a room and
> doing all of these team-building kinds of things.

Everyone pulls names out of a hat to share a room. But once, we got into this kind of a "girl" thing, where, literally, people were saying "Well, I want to room with such and such and I want to room with —," and of course no one grabbed me to share a room with, and I didn't grab anyone to share a room with either. So I wound up staying in a room on my own, which was fine on one hand, but on the other hand, I felt really terrible that no one wanted to share a room with me. But then it flips back around to me thinking, "Well I'm not going to care. I'll be just fine. I'm not going to reach out to them either. I'll watch television and pretend I'm home," because that's what I really want to do anyway. But it still feels bad.

It's fine when you're in control of it, but then you really feel as if you've been excommunicated, and that does not feel so great. I feel as if I'm not being appreciated. My manager never asked me who I roomed with, so she never realized that I didn't room with anyone. I felt neglected, but I think they neglect me because they feel I don't need attention. They feel I'm fine with it.

Cecilia is first and foremost an entertainer:

My introversion has held me back not only in marketing but in my music career as well. This too might be a cultural thing. And a lot of my introversion comes out of my insecurity. As said earlier, I can just sit in a corner doing my thing, but I need to be coaxed out. I can write a million letters to a million record companies asking if they accept tapes, but to follow up and call them becomes impossible. I lack the confidence to say, "I'm great; you better listen to me." The introvert in me does not really believe that. And no one is going to call *me* up and say they are interested in what I'm doing. I'm the leader of the band, but that's only because everyone else is so lazy. I'm very good at getting things done, and I can get really fixated on results. And even though we're working, we're not getting paid. *I* call up the clubs. *I* get the gigs. But I'm *not* good at networking with other musicians, widening my pool of other people to play with. As a result, other musicians do not call me saying, "Do you want to be on this bill?" And I don't know whether it's because they don't like my music or because they don't think I'm a very friendly person.

Music is very cliquey, like other industries, and a lot depends on who likes you. I don't find it easy to break into the clique because I'm stuck in the "Oh, I don't want to bother them" syndrome, rather than going out there and doing the "hail fellow, well met." To be successful in this industry, I feel you need endless friends and acquaintances. And if I'm really good, everyone will like me for my music and then they will automatically call. Of course, I know they won't. It's really all about your networking abilities.

Actually, I do initiate a number of contacts, but all of the people are very individualistic themselves, instead of being really connected.

These are some really good points, which help paint a picture of many introverts' overall patterns.

But what about when Cecilia is on stage? How does that feel? I asked her.

My best shows are when I have done my mental preparation. I have riled myself and said, "This is going to be really good." But I get very distracted by what's going on in the audience. And there is a lot of internal noise. In fact, it took a lot of time before I really felt comfortable on stage. When I first started, I would feel physically sick. Now I get on the stage and feel that I've done a lot of preparation and I'm ready. I can't see myself not performing. I started performing in America five years ago. My first performance was about eight years ago, in England. And it was a disaster. When I came out with a regular band five years ago, it was awful, awful, awful for about a year and a half.

But then I forced myself to go solo, and once the solo performing became easier the band was a piece of cake. By going solo, I put myself in a horrific situation. It's the hardest thing to do, because when I'm performing, I'm very exposed, not just because I'm alone, but because I'm singing *my* songs, which are about times in *my* life—so it's pretty raw. A lot of my songs are quite personal. They're all feelings or thoughts about feeling isolated, rejected, left, all those introverted things we've talked about. Solo is naked. Then I realized the only way to improve my performance was to hang out a lot more than I was and play out on my own. Those two things increased my confidence and familiarity with the situation. And if you can do it when you are naked, then you can do it when you have clothes on—that is, with a band. Masked. With a band.

So, the introversion and the isolation actually impact my songwriting and my performance, and the way in which I do them. And now I've moved from being in a band to being a solo performer to being the leader of the band. As the leader I am in an isolated position, and the band members are the team. The musicians I'm working with, at the moment, all consider themselves not a part of me. So, many times, when solo artists with bands get record contracts, unless the band has a really unique quality, the record company might fire the band and just keep the singer. There is no reason for the band to think they are in it for the long haul. Unlike in companies, if I do well, the band may or may not get to stay.

It is very easy for a company to replace the band members. And it's very easy to subtract *me* out of the equation, which leads to a certain amount of uncertainty and discomfort on the part of the band. The band can easily say, "We want to be paid, or, we want a certain percentage of your songs." For example, I put down that they wrote say, 25 percent of the song, and you can then negotiate on publishing rights. And *publishing* is the only place where I actually stand to make money. It all gets very technical and has to be negotiated. If I wrote the song, why should I pay someone else 25 percent of my work. Lennon and McCartney shared their songwriting credits with the publishers, even though you know very clearly which ones are John's and which ones are Paul's. But they were two seventeen-year-old lads in school. I'm not in that situation. I'm getting older, and I need to protect what I have and at the same time negotiate what's best for all concerned. My introversion makes it difficult. I need to make the band a team, but how do I do that? How do you say, "This is my song; this is all you get"? That's my dilemma because I hate business- or money-related type conversations. But I have to protect my interests!

I had an agency, but I think they did not do $6,000 worth of work. I think, maybe, they did $600 worth of work. So how do I have that conversation? After being coached, I hope that I will be able to have this kind of conversation up front. For introverts, when things become clearer, having those conversations will be easier. But meanwhile, I just hate those conversations. I know that there are people who really rise to the challenge. They love the art of negotiation; they thrive on asking themselves, "How can I get the most bang for the buck." But I feel as if I'm taking advantage of them. So, I'd rather sit home. This is not at all good business sense.

After thinking about wanting to have business conversations up front, I realize that today, with my band, I do now try to negotiate up front. I ask, "How do you want to be paid? And when do you want to be paid?" If their answer does not work for me, I tell them what I can do and they can leave or they can stay, but at least now it's clear.

And there have been situations where people will backtrack from our original conversation, and then I need to learn to stick to my guns. I tend to get worried that the friendship will be ruined. And I hate being taken advantage of. And though I think

I'm a *very* fair person, I can't stand anyone feeling that I'm taking advantage of them, so this is how I end up offering to pay half of what the disagreement is about, which pacifies me, but I pay money that I really don't feel I owe. A band member who is extroverted and more vocal than I am can really get over. And right now, there is a bass player from Nashville who is playing with me on Thursday night. I was not even sure I wanted him, but he not only talked his way into playing, but also into getting paid up front. How did this happen? How am I going to get out of this one? The reality is it shouldn't even be a dialogue. I should have just been able to say, "No, I don't want you to play with me (on Thursday night). Thanks very much." But I couldn't say that.

The Path to Change

Two years ago Julia left her job as a senior analyst for an insurance company to become the assistant director of a small not-for-profit theater company—a *major* career change!

"I always felt as if I had a more difficult time talking to people and asking people for things, even as a kid," she recalled, when thinking about her feelings as an adult and as a child. "At home I was considered just 'regular.' I guess that's because I have evolved from a very introverted family."

Thinking about how her introversion affects her interaction with her family and friends today, Julia said:

I never confront people with what I'm thinking. And this obviously affects my management. Again, I come from an introverted family. And I still have a hard time with this. It's always a struggle. I feel as if I just don't have the energy. I feel that it is just easier to do everything myself rather than ask anyone to help me with a project. With friends, I am not as horrid. The introversion impacts me more at work, but I do deal with it daily, also, with family and friends.

I think Julia's last statement is very interesting—the fact that she feels her introversion impacts her life at work more so than with her family and friends. And this is why this book is meant to delve into and address the introvert's work environment. But, as with the others, I asked Julia to think about her home and family, when she was growing up. Was her shyness or introversion supported? Perhaps this is why she feels less threatened by her introversion away from her job.

Julia went on to tell how she now realizes that everyone in her family was introverted. And Julia's young nieces and nephew seem to behave exactly the same way Julia did when she was growing up. Their school, for example, reports that the children are quiet. "The teachers *think* that there is something going on within those brains, but they're not sure what," says Julia, the empathetic aunt.

Julia also explained that she doesn't really think that her introversion was supported by her family, because they were all the same. So she imagines them all saying, "Oh my God, we have to go outside now." And Julia thinks she learned this type of behavior from her family.

My mother would not take us to the doctor unless we were really sick. She did not want to bother him with anything frivolous. It had to be something definitely wrong. And when we got to the doctor, our symptoms had better be the same as she had described over the phone, because of her fear that the doctor would say "I don't know why you're here . . ." Since I think my whole family is like this, I guess maybe we did support one another, but in an unhealthy way. If I said "I don't want to go outside to talk to that person," my mother would say, "Oh I know how you feel. I don't want to speak to that person either."

I shared with Julia that my parents, on the other hand, forced me to go out, when I really wanted to stay home and read.

Well in my case when I wanted to stay home and watch television, my mother didn't care. But I put pressure on myself, because somehow I knew it was weird. When my sister was outside running with the neighborhood kids, I knew I needed to do that too. But I preferred to stay home, reading books and watching TV.

I asked Julia why she left her native California for "extroverted" New York.

I went to school in California for a year and then thought I'd come to New York to pursue an acting career. Acting was a way for me to be extroverted without feeling self-conscious. I went to New York University and majored in theater, but then it became really difficult for me to go to auditions. I just could not do it. So I returned to school for an M.B.A. in finance. I don't know why. It just seemed like a safe thing to do.

As for Julia's workplace, I asked how comfortable she felt in the meetings at her current job or socially with her coworkers. She said that she is *really* comfortable, now, in her position as assistant director of her theater company:

> *I* call the meetings and set the agenda. In the past, when I was at the insurance company, I was very uncomfortable and tried very hard not to talk. If I *had* to talk, I could only do so if I felt strongly about something. I would contribute if it was brainstorming and I felt very strongly about an issue. It had to hit me. In a meeting with just my peers I can talk.
>
> Finding this position at the theater company was the most difficult thing I have ever done in my life, because I had to sell myself. Selling the company to funders and potential donors is fun! I have a much easier time, since I'm involved with the fund-raising. I can sell the company, because everyone is depending on me for money, and I guess I can hide behind the company. However, in functions outside of work, I am really not comfortable. I don't want small talk. I will go, but I don't have a good time. And it was really a struggle at the insurance company. I always thought it was a nightmare.

Julia further explained that her introversion, until now, has really held her back in certain ways in her career.

At the insurance company, I never knew how to act, or what to say, or how to assert myself. I had never really had a real career until this new position. I "hung out" at work. A real career was not defined. I didn't fit in, and I took so much of what happened there personally. Yes, my introversion held me back at the insurance company, and I probably would still be there if I didn't get some career counseling and guidance. I could have died there. I *was* dying there. I had no idea where to go, but I knew I was desperately unhappy. Defining my goals and merging my values and interests with my skills really allowed me to see what a terrible fit I was in that environment and how much happier I would be in the world of theater. I just didn't know how to take the first step, and networking was so foreign to me.

Taking all of the assessment instruments during my job search really helped me clarify issues in terms of past promotions and career success. I thought it was very valuable. And everyone, all of my friends, describe me as an extrovert. But I describe myself as a *loud* introvert. Part of it is that my voice is so loud. But to hear confirmation that in fact I am an introvert is very *comforting* for me. The MBTI clarified my introversion for me. And that it's OK to be an introvert. It told me that there are other people like me. And it's a relief! I still get angry with myself, I still can't fully accept it, but I do know that people survive cocktail parties. It's not the end of the world.

Part of me feels that extroverts have easier lives. Although I guess there are some introverts that don't worry so much about being shy or introverted. I wish *I could* "get out there." I wish it weren't so hard for me.

When the concept of networking was proposed to me my first feeling was pure nausea and terrible anxiety. This was just because I thought I couldn't do it. I thought I was physically and mentally unable to do it. It is a real self-consciousness. You have to put yourself out there. You have to "go outside." You have to stop watching television, pull up the blinds, and go outside. And then you have to ask someone something, and then ask them for a favor. And then you have to show up. I wish there were a script to follow. At least I had a general script. I knew I wasn't getting any younger. So I asked myself, "What's the worst that's going to happen?" I'm not going to die. The worst that could happen is they won't call me back, or they'll tell me I'm a pest. The best that could happen is that they'll agree to see me. But then of course I'd have to show up. In the larger-than-life sense of consequence, there was really nothing that could happen to me. But I'd have to be in a talking mode to do it. If I was not in "talking mode" there was simply no way, on this earth, in this life, on this planet that I was going to be able to do this.

My introversion now affects my interaction with *my* board of directors, because I've changed careers from the private sector to the not-for-profit sector. Instead of one boss I have twelve board members! Surprisingly, it's working out. It's actually nice to have a board to report to and to be in an industry that I love. The board is very supportive.

Before the career change, I believe my introversion really affected my performance in the office. Now, with this job, as the assistant director, even when we have a fund-raising function and I have to shmooze and booze—and I guess that is the part of the job I dislike the most—I'm dealing with it.

Since Julia had totally changed careers, she took courses in arts management at NYU, which proved beneficial. And, most of all, she had to make a commitment to change. Her finance background helped a lot, too. And all of the work that we did, which took a very long time—two years—*really paid off*. Julia learned that career change is a process; it cannot happen overnight. Julia now works in a totally new environment. And she feels as if she has finally found her "center," as she puts it.

When was the last time Julia did some networking? And, as we narrowed and defined her targets and she developed a passion for her new career, did the networking process become easier for Julia?

"I now network all of the time for fund-raising purposes," Julia responded. "I'm not sure I feel any more comfortable with it than I did initially, but I do it with such purpose." Julia finally has a target about which she feels passionate. According to her, things are not so ominous. She is determined to be the most credible arts manager out there. "I was on a mission. I had to get into this field, and I knew it was a fit for me," she proudly declared.

Julia speaks of her career change as a process. The exercises in this book will help *you*, too, with this rewarding process and wonderful journey.

Finding Your Passion

It seems that a key element that enables introverts to cope *better* with networking is when they view networking as a necessary step toward fulfilling their true passion, or to achieve a specific purpose. The euphoria derived from reaching the summit overrides the steep process or journey of getting there. So, it appears that when we discover our true purpose in life— our destiny—then reaching that destiny, by any means necessary, becomes the focus and a compensating factor.

Do you remember the transformation that took place with Stacey? We discovered her passion—the sports industry—and she confirmed that things have continued to turn around for her ever since we narrowed and defined her job-area choices, or targets. Stacey developed a passion for the industry she truly saw herself in:

> With sports being my target industry, networking has become, and is becoming, easier—partly by luck. And I believe everyone has some luck, and because of the luck I've been able to travel the path. I've been trying to get into the sports industry for a very long time—for years. And now it is really starting to happen. I'm talking to the right people, and even though they may not have a job for me now, they are referring me on, and they may also remember me further down the road themselves. I'm finally stepping in the right direction, and it feels good, especially when I get good feedback.
>
> Here's an example of what I mean: My boss was going on and on about how we don't want to get involved in the sports world because it's male dominated and there are instances of violence towards women. She felt, "Why would we want to put money into that?" That made me really angry, and my introversion prevented me from saying anything to her. But I'm going to write up a two-page paper,

and in many places I'll agree with her, because she's right on a lot of levels, but the reality is there are very few real winners in the sports industry. Aside from the men behind the scenes who control the purse strings, everybody loses, especially the players. I will write about that in my paper. One of my goals is to change the way we think about the industry. Everything will get funneled into my paper.

Earlier, I pointed out that it's easier for introverts to write than to speak, but we can clearly see that Stacey is finally coming into her own. And who knows? As she becomes even more involved with her true passion, and more confident, maybe she will increasingly verbalize some of the positions she writes about in her paper.

As all of these interviews reveal, introverts can successfully fulfill a wide range of careers, from lawyer to musician, as long as they discover their passion and become aware of how to accept and accommodate their own patterns and preferences. Introversion can actually become an asset instead of a liability.

Take a look at Lenny Kravitz, the R & B/soul music artist, for example. Some critics have claimed that because Kravitz prefers to go into the recording studio alone and play all the instruments himself instead of collaborating with other musicians, he has deprived himself of becoming a superstar along the lines of Madonna or Prince. Kravitz also tends to shy away from interviews and to wear mirrored glasses at all times to protect himself from what he perceives to be a prying public. But although he may not have achieved cult status, no one can argue that Kravitz isn't practicing his passion. And he guards his right to follow that passion the way he knows he must. "It's like a painting. You wouldn't say to a painter, 'Why don't you get a group of artists to paint with you?'" says Kravitz (McCormick 1998).

Recognizing your passion and accepting your introversion can ultimately lead to a successful career in which you'll find yourself doing and saying things you never dreamed possible. As Stacey said of her own introverted family, the only time they truly step out of their introversion is when they are practicing their passion.

6

MANAGING INTROVERTS

"Never let the fear of striking out get in your way."
BABE RUTH

"Management has to do with the way information gets filtered to others," says Elizabeth Westell, an extroverted manager at a large bank. "An extrovert tends to convey information through interaction, but it's not the style of an introvert to take in information that way. So, when an extrovert wants to approach their boss or their subordinate with a problem or with an idea, they would like it to be unscheduled, spontaneous, and interactive. An introverted employee or manager needs time to think about it."

If you are an introvert that is either managed by someone else or managing others, you can use positive self-realization, career-management strategies, and workplace-survival techniques to uncover your distinct assets and power. Maybe you haven't realized the power that you have, but many a smart manager will creatively tailor or adapt their management style when working with introverts and extroverts so that their work environment will reflect the best of all worlds. Introverts, their staff, and the managers they report to can capitalize on this. And the managers cited in this chapter superbly demonstrate this.

79

Some of the managers I've interviewed are well versed in Personality Types; therefore, I am providing you with some MBTI language to assist you throughout this chapter.

The following tables, taken from Paul D. Tieger and Barbara Baron-Tieger's *The Personality Type Tool Kit**, explain and help interpret the various personality types to which the managers refer. This chapter also concludes with another excerpt from the *Tool Kit* and a discussion of its application to introverted management.

There are four dimensions of personality type, and the first has to do with extroversion** and its opposite, introversion. The Personality Type model is based on four basic aspects of human personality: how we interact with the world and where we direct our energy; the kind of information we naturally notice and remember; how we make decisions; and whether we prefer to live in a more structured or more spontaneous way. We call these aspects of human personality *dimensions* because each one can be viewed as a continuum between opposite extremes, like this:

How we interact with the world and where we direct our energy

Extroversion (E) ←————————→ Introversion (I)

Extroverts	Introverts
Focus attention outward	Focus attention inward
Enjoy a variety of tasks	Work best on one project at a time

---

*Reprinted with permission from the authors. All rights reserved. Modified and reproduced by special permission of the Publisher, Consulting Psychologists Press, Inc., Palo Alto, Calif. 94303, from *Introduction to Type, Fifth Edition* by Isabel Briggs Myers. Copyright 1993 by Consulting Psychologists Press, Inc. All rights reserved. Further reproduction is prohibited without the Publisher's written consent.

***The Personality Type Tool Kit* utilizes the Jungian spelling, "extravert," but for consistency, the alternate spelling is used here and throughout the book.

Extroverts (continued)	Introverts (continued)
Seek out and need other people	Enjoy tasks that require concentration
Work at a rapid pace	Work at a careful, steady pace
Need to talk about ideas to think them through	Consider things fully before responding

The kind of information we naturally notice and remember

Sensing (S)  Intuition (N)

Sensors	Intuitives
Focus on "what is"	Focus on "what could be"
Like working with real things	Enjoy theory and speculation
Apply past experience to solving problems	Like working with possibilities and implications
Need specific and realistic directions	Need to use imagination

How we make decisions

Thinking (T) ← → Feeling (F)

Thinkers	Feelers
Enjoy analyzing problems logically	Need work to be personally meaningful
Make fair and objective decisions	Like helping others and being appreciated
Need to weigh the pros and cons to make decisions	Need decisions to be congruent with values
Can be tough negotiators	Need to work in a friendly environment
	Are driven to understand others and contribute

Whether we prefer to live in a more structured or in a more spontaneous way

Judging (J) ← → Perceiving (P)	
Judgers	**Perceivers**
Enjoy work that allows them to make decisions	Enjoy flexible and changing work situations
Prefer a predictable work pattern and environment	Like to be able to respond to problems as they arise
Work toward completing their responsibilities before relaxing	Are more satisfied with fewer rules and procedures
Like to maintain control of their projects	Need to have fun in their work

The four dimensions lead to 16 different types (as seen below). For further work in determining which type you are, you may want to do additional work with a qualified Myers-Briggs counselor.

ISTJ

Introvert, Sensing, Thinking, Judging

Serious and quiet. Earns success by concentration and thoroughness. Practical, orderly, matter-of-fact, logical, realistic, and dependable. Sees to it that everything is well organized. Takes responsibility. Makes up own mind as to what should be accomplished and works toward it steadily, regardless of protests or distractions.

ISFJ

Introvert, Sensing, Feeling, Judging

Quiet, friendly, responsible, and conscientious. Works devotedly to meet obligations. Lends stability to any project or group. Thorough and painstakingly accurate. Interests are usually not technical. Can be patient with necessary details. Loyal, considerate, perceptive, concerned with how other people feel.

INFJ

Introvert, Intuitive, Feeling, Judging

Succeeds by perseverance, originality, and desire to do whatever is needed or wanted. Put best efforts into their work. Quietly forceful, conscientious, concerned for others. Respected for firm principles. Likely to be honored and followed for clear visions as to how to best serve the common good.

INTJ

Introvert, Intuitive, Thinking, Judging

Original mind and great drive for own ideas and purposes. Long-range vision; quickly finds meaningful patterns in external events. In appealing fields, organizes a job and carries it through. Skeptical, critical, independent, and determined; high standards of competence and performance.

ISTP

Introvert, Sensing, Thinking, Perceiving

Cool onlooker—quiet, reserved, observing and analyzing life with detached curiosity and unexpected flashes of original humor. Usually interested in cause and effect, how and why mechanical things work, and in organizing facts, using logical principles. Excels at getting to the core of a practical problem and finding the solution.

ISFP

Introvert, Sensing, Feeling, Perceiving

Retiring, quietly friendly, sensitive, kind, modest about abilities. Shuns disagreements, does not force opinions or values on others. Usually does not care to lead but is often a loyal follower. Often relaxed about getting things done. Enjoys the present moment and does not want to spoil it by undue haste or exertion.

INFP

Introvert, Intuitive, Feeling, Perceiving

Quiet observer, idealistic, loyal. Important that outer life be congruent with inner values. Curious, quick to see possibilities, often serves as catalyst to implement ideas. Adaptable, flexible, and accepting, unless a value is threatened. Wants to understand people and ways of fulfilling human potential. Little concern with possessions or surroundings.

INTP

Introvert, Intuitive, Thinking, Perceiving

Quiet and reserved. Especially enjoys theoretical or scientific pursuits. Likes solving problems with logic and analysis. Interested mainly in ideas, with little liking for parties or small talk. Tends to have sharply defined interests. Needs a career in which some strong interests can be used and useful.

ESTP

Extrovert, Sensing, Thinking, Perceiving

Good at on-the-spot problem solving. Likes action; enjoys whatever comes along. Tends to like mechanical things and sports, with friends on the side. Adaptable, tolerant, pragmatic; focused on getting results. Dislikes long explanations. Best with real things that can be worked on, handled, taken apart, or put together.

ESFP

Extrovert, Sensing, Feeling, Perceiving

Outgoing, accepting, friendly, enjoys everything and makes things more fun for others by their enjoyment. Likes action and making things happen. Knows what's going on and joins in eagerly. Finds remembering facts easier than mastering theories. Is best in situations that need sound common sense and practical ability with people.

ENFP

Extrovert, Intuitive, Feeling, Perceiving

Warmly enthusiastic, high-spirited, ingenious, imaginative. Able to do almost anything of interest. Quick with a solution for any difficulty and ready to help anybody with a problem. Often relies on ability to improvise instead of preparing in advance. Can usually find compelling reasons for satisfying wants.

ENTP

Extrovert, Intuitive, Thinking, Perceiving

Quick, ingenious, good at many things. Stimulating company, alert, and outspoken. May argue for fun on either side of a question. Resourceful in solving new and challenging problems, but may neglect routine assignments. Apt to turn to one new interest after another. Skillful in finding logical reasons for satisfying wants.

ESTJ

Extrovert, Sensing, Thinking, Judging

Practical, realistic, matter-of-fact, with a natural head for business or mechanics. Not interested in abstract theories; wants learning to have direct and immediate application. Likes to organize and run activities. Often good administrator; is decisive; quickly moves to implement decisions and takes care of routine details.

ESFJ

Extrovert, Sensing, Feeling, Judging

Warm-hearted, talkative, popular, conscientious, born cooperator, active committee member. Needs harmony and may be good at creating it. Always doing something nice for someone. Works best with encouragement and praise. Main interest is in things that directly and visibly affect people's lives.

ENFJ

Extrovert, Intuitive, Feeling, Judging

Responsive and responsible. Feels real concern for what others think or want, and tries to handle things with due regard for others' feelings. Can present a proposal or lead a group discussion with ease and tact. Sociable, popular, sympathetic. Responsive to praise and criticism. Likes to facilitate others and enable people to achieve their potential.

ENTJ

Extrovert, Intuitive, Thinking, Judging

Frank and decisive; leader in activities. Develops and implements comprehensive systems to solve organizational problems. Good at anything that requires reasoning and intelligent talk, such as public speaking. Is usually well-informed and enjoys learning new things.

Of course, you aren't going to absorb all of this MBTI information immediately—but use it as a continued reference. Now, let's return to Elizabeth.

Elizabeth and I spoke about viewing introverts as assets or liabilities within her company. She explained that she strongly feels that it depends on what kind of job introverts are in:

> If they are in a data-gathering or strategic-thinking type job, or if they are introverts that are trying to get something done, I think they are highly valued. I don't think there is a differentiation between introverts and extroverts who are in the right job. A lot of extroverts in the kinds of jobs that introverts do well would fail, or would not do them as well, such as data gathering and strategic planning. Introverts are very much involved in get-

ting the process done. They make great process managers and great operations managers. Here, they can look a lot like extroverts because they have such a desire to "do it." So I think it depends on the type of job and the type of introvert we're talking about. There are certain types of introverts that are not going to be highly valued by organizations. But any introvert in the right slot, using their skills, is going to take in information and think about it and come out with meaningful conclusions—be it meaningful actions, meaningful analyses, meaningful strategies, or meaningful program development. I can think of four or five introverts just off the top of my head who are doing very well in the jobs they are in. And they are all different, and the jobs very much suit them.

A person who is an introvert in a job doing credit policy, policy making, policy dissemination, considering the grand scheme of policy and credit, teaching a small group about credit concepts, thinking about the future and necessity of credit—all of those big-picture jobs fit introverts well. Yet even though introverts share many traits, the introverts that have reported to me were all very different. The "sensing" aspect of introverted sensors helps a lot when communicating with an extrovert. One of my direct reports, Brenda, was an ISTJ (Introvert, Sensing, Thinking, Judging)—she was a real get-it-done person. As it related to me, she could take her data-gathering sensing and her thinking and put it together to figure out what I needed from her and what she needed from me; she created a balance of information-sharing that worked for both of us. We complemented each other. The same with Cynthia, another of the folks who reported to me. She was also an IS. She could see the world in the moment. She had the ability to see and process something in a way that made sense so that we could feed it back to the outside world—and have it make sense for them.

Introverted intuitives are more difficult for me to manage, because so much of what is going on is intuitive. Introverted intuitives think in the future, not the here and now—and they don't communicate the future. Introverted sensors can better communicate to an extroverted manager whatever it is they are trying to do. As a manager, that's what one needs to know. What is somebody doing? With an introverted intuitive, in order to bring out the best in that person, you must acknowledge the differences. I need to talk about what I don't understand, what I am not getting and be able to "hear" from the other person why that is difficult. The best solution is to bring it out in the open, in private and in a comfortable setting, where you can talk about your working relationship. I discuss what they need to hear from me and what I need to hear from them.

It's comparable to a marriage, in a way. In fact I'm married to an introvert, so I've always been aware of introversion as a type. I'll tell you how I handled a recent "management with an introverted employee" situation.

I was in California, at an off-site event with David, an introvert. I brought him in as a consultant, so I was responsible for him. We get along and communicate very well—but there has always been some kind of gap in our different communication styles. It's like a time lapse. Things in San Francisco were not going well. The three-day seminar we had been hired to teach had some serious problems. I was sure that David was worried. I was certainly worried. In fact he was probably more worried than I was, but there was that time lapse, again, between when I was fully aware that he was worried, and when I was worried. I woke up at five o'clock in the morning and called him and said, "This entire week could be a disaster if we don't do something! This is not going well!" Now, he already was aware of that, and in fact, had made some major corrections to our presentation. But an extrovert does have a "bias to action" that I don't think introverts have. Introverts are still mulling it over. I wanted to physically do something, and David wanted to think about it. I don't think we ever discussed that aspect of it, but clearly that was creating tension between us. He *was* doing something, but he was doing it internally— therefore my perception was that he was doing "nothing." I wanted to actively and physically *do* something. I wanted to write up sheets, I wanted to talk about it, I wanted to think about it out loud, *I wanted to physically do something!* When I say "bias to action," whether he was thinking or not, I needed to see him doing something physical. In this instance, thinking about it was not physical. Thinking is not acting, no matter what anyone says. It means doing something actively, and that is different from thinking about it.

"This may very well be an area where introverts trip themselves up in organizations," I told Elizabeth. "An introvert acts *without* that process of *doing*, and the perception is that we are not taking charge. There is no process there. I have learned to 'push back' and say 'I am working on it.'"

Elizabeth further explained:

> My perception of David in this instance was that he
> was not acting—he was thinking—and that is a
> whole different process. Thinking is not acting. He
> was not taking action. It got resolved when he came
> to breakfast and we talked about it and tried a couple
> of things. It turned out that the entire off-site
> presentation really was not terribly successful in the
> long run. But at any rate, we muddled through it.
>
> You know, I'd like to think that I am capable of
> altering my management style when interacting
> with introverts, but I'm not sure I do it consciously.
> For instance, when I went on a business trip, I left
> Brenda (the ISTJ) "in charge." She wrote down
> everything that happened during my absence, and
> it was very helpful. But when I returned, and mes-
> sages and mail had piled up, it was too much infor-
> mation for me to absorb. I could not get through
> it, even though I wanted to know it all. So when
> we talked about it, I asked Brenda, "Is there any
> way you could give me an overview first?" She said,
> "Well, I can't give it to you first, but I can continue
> to write down everything, then I can look at it and
> extract the pertinent points." Then she would put
> those pertinent points in the margin, after she had
> written it all down. That gave me all of the infor-
> mation I needed, which I could then choose to read
> or not read. And we talked about that. I had really
> been overwhelmed initially by the amount of infor-
> mation that she gave me. But this made it more
> manageable.
>
> Extroverted managers have to do more explor-
> ing of what works with introverts. You have to talk

about it if you are an extroverted manager, because introverts won't necessarily discuss it. As an extroverted manager, you have to make a point of reaching out to your introverts. Have regular conversations until you get it right. Once you get it right, you won't have trouble.

Now extroverted managers might not have a clue as to what to look for to determine introversion in their employees. However, if you look for someone who generally keeps a lower profile, you'll know they have some potential toward introversion. It's absolutely important to help introverts to further develop professionally in the workplace, and again, we would do that by talking about their needs and the needs of the manager. To get introverts networking, for example, have them start with their very best friends, and best friends of best friends. The introverts who have had trouble networking could do it if they perceived it as having intimate conversations with friends about their dreams and future. It just goes slowly; you can't make them do it fast.

Emily, another extroverted manager, also in banking and consulting, adds to Elizabeth's convictions:

I think the introverts that are perceived the most positively have found ways to creatively work with managers who are extroverted so that they themselves are perceived as being more extroverted—something like a "secret weapon." These people always have a take on things; they always have something else to say about situations around the organization. These introverts build such a strong rapport with the person that the extroverts pay a lot of attention to what they say. Introverts need to pay a lot of attention, though, to who they are speaking with, who's on the other side of the table. Because if they have not attended to those rapport issues, they can wind up in trouble. Most of the world is extroverted, especially in New York City, so you need to find a lot of extroverted ways of behaving. The introverts that I have worked with use the word shy, or quiet, when they describe themselves. When we examine their behavior and we do the MBTI, I think they feel a tremendous relief when they realize they are introverts. Especially when they are not psychologically minded at all. Someone who I am working with now, who will need a lot of coaching, has always counted on her extroverted managers to intercede for her. She now has a manager who is an attorney and will not do this for her. As a result, she finds herself becoming quite needy and dependent on other people. She will attempt to take on leadership roles, but then gets very nervous in the negotiation process. She is someone who will have a difficult time being valued, so coaching is in order, to help her learn how to use her introversion in a positive way.

Right now, she demonstrates extroverted behavior when you first meet her—a sometimes adolescent quality that can be inappropriate. Where her introversion comes out is not always clear. She does not totally own her introversion and fails to recognize that it could be used as a strength. She appears, at times, to be immature. But managers can single out introverts in a positive way. A smart and perceptive introvert can listen, watch, and carefully select their spoken words. I don't think they are discounted more than the extrovert. The challenge for the introvert, in order for them to be effective, is to do more extroverted kinds of things, in order for them to be perceived as valuable. Introverts need to develop extroverted kinds of behaviors that are comfortable for them. They should "wear them" until they get comfortable with those behaviors.

Often, when working with an introverted client, I encourage them to take little baby steps, because little baby steps are better than no steps at all. It's like going to Weight Watchers. When Weight Watcher clients whine because they only lost half a pound, the group leader asks if they would like that half pound back. Introverts can thrive and grow on little victories just like that half pound. Afraid to pick up the phone? Write that person a letter first, informing him you will be calling in a week. Now you *have* to follow up! And you'll have your first small victory. There are times when that one small victory can get us started on a roll. We can't think of it as an entire project. We can only think, "One small step for mankind."

Emily continued with her description of the introvert:

I feel I can pretty much tell whether or not an employee is introverted, although I generally don't start out assessing people that way. I try to be a little bit more *tabula rasa*, if I can. I start by asking questions, and I ask them to start talking about their strengths. I want to find out what *they* see as valuable within themselves. And sometimes even extroverts have difficulty doing that. When managing an introvert, I do a lot of "What would happen if . . ." When they tell me that this process is not going to be very easy for them, I congratulate them for being able to say that—that they already know that part of themselves. I say: Let's try on a bunch of different things and see what might be the most comfortable for you. New shoes are not going to be comfy when you first buy them. So let's go shopping and see if we can find something that you like.

Offer introverts a range of things to do. Ask: Have there been situations in your life where you just found yourself talking to a stranger? What was the situation? What was it like? Did you come away with any information? I personally enjoy networking. It's something that I do easily. So, I want to tell others to "just do it," because I love it so much. Finding a way to say this is not rocket science. But we need to find a way that's easy for them. I have the power to say that. Introverts need to manage their introversion the way extroverts need to manage their extroversion. And managing *my* extroversion is *not* easy! I know I have a lot of energy that can be overwhelming for an introvert, so, frequently, I find that when I am talking to introverts, I tend to look away. I try not to stare at them because it makes them uncomfortable. I know that I have very strong eye contact and I have to manage that. I have learned to back off, after I have charged ahead pretty far. I say to introverts: "In case you have not noticed, I tend to be pretty enthusiastic about things." I use humor a lot to explain differences, especially if I can use the humor against myself.

"Have *you* ever reported to an introvert?" I asked.

Early in my career I had an introverted boss. She was very detail conscious. And I was new in the group. I think she wanted to mentor and develop me, but she was not comfortable talking to me about things that I was interested in. She would ask me to do a memo and then she would dissect it to death. It may have been a way for us to spend time together, but for me, it was excruciating. I would get crazed. She would drive me crazy and it was hard to relate to her. I did not know what to do to relate to her, and I really struggled. It was a real style issue. In social relationships, she was not smooth, although she was respected as someone who was very smart. Her smarts got her promoted in the organization, but she was going only but so far and no further. The introversion got in her way, but she did not have a skill deficit. It was that she was shy. She had been in the military and that style fit her quite well. I believe my energy must have gotten in the way. She pushed back, and her way of controlling my interaction was to pick at the little details.

The other introvert I reported to was a man who hired me in advertising. Again, I think he hired me as a protégé. He had worked in the Peace Corps. He did a lot of hiring of women and minorities before affirmative action. I had to make a presentation on the executive floor, and he made me do it about twice a day in front of him. Needless to say, I was terrified. I got through the experience. But again, it was a way of relating to me in a picky way, because I had too much energy. In a good way, I became his mouthpiece. If he needed to tell the people in the mailroom something, he would send me.

I consider both of these people as my sponsors, and they share interesting patterns. They perceived a deficit in themselves. They could rise and be promoted, but I think they wanted me to go out and "fill in" the piece they felt was missing in themselves. Which is actually the way people *should* hire other people.

Carolyn, the introverted "always performing" attorney, said: "I do not delegate. I'm clear, but I'd rather do it myself. When I do delegate, I'm standing over you. I am the worst kind of manager, everyone's nightmare—a micromanager. I am not going to trust that you are just going to get the job done. And I'm very condescending. But at my last job, where both of my assistants were introverted, we actually got along well. I let them stretch. And I *did* trust their decisions. In fact, my entire staff was introverted, and we had a really good time."

Julia, the introverted financial analyst who became executive director of a theater company, feels her management style is getting better. "I have a staff made up of introverts and extroverts. My problem is that I have a tendency to assume that people know what I'm thinking about, and they really do not have a clue. Then I have a temper tantrum because my needs have not been met. With coaching, I'm learning to be clearer with my staff. The theater productions have become better as well. Although I am still in a learning curve, things are so much clearer."

And Emily really helped to clear things up; she hit it on the mark when she said, "The challenge for the introvert—

for them to be effective—is that they need to do more extroverted kinds of things in order to be perceived as being valuable."

Elizabeth talks about extroverts wanting to be spontaneous and interactive and introverts needing time to think:

> You have to give introverts enough of a warning and enough information. You should say something like: "I'd like a meeting at noon to talk about some problems with the budget, and here is some pre-meeting information so that when we meet we can talk about it." Extroverts have to learn how to do that, and even when they learn *how* to do it, it's a real pain. It's a pain for an extrovert to have to schedule something. They want to talk about the here and now, and they want it solved now. They are, probably, in the middle of thinking about something and want the information now, not tomorrow at three o'clock, but now. But introverts, when approaching their manager and acting less spontaneous, for example, want to stop, take more time to analyze and then say (still thinking it through): "Is this the right direction—that I'm going in?" Or, "Can you take a look at this and give me some feedback?" Or, "I came to this part and I'm fine up until here, but I'm not comfortable moving forward because I need your input on this."
>
> As I said, extroverts want everything here and now; they do not want to wait. They don't want to write something down, plan for a meeting and be put on somebody's calendar. But this is the reality of business. You have to get on somebody's calendar, and as an extroverted manager, I was one to always be available to talk to somebody about something at

almost any given moment. I could do that. I could at least ask for more information and bounce off ideas, and if there was something I needed more information about I would say, "I'm not comfortable with this and this and this, so get me more." But an introverted manager may not even want to deal with it at that moment. So it becomes a learning experience for an extroverted (I-need-your-feedback-now) subordinate, and it's not a comfortable learning experience.

Extroverts Reporting to Introverts

If you are an extrovert reporting to an introverted manager, there are some important factors to take into account when considering how much information they require from you and how often. As Elizabeth's experience will relay, introverted managers often expect you to foresee their needs, don't require much feedback as long as you get the job done, and don't offer much feedback, either, even when you are doing a good job.

Introverted managers tend to really leave you alone and in some cases, in some strange way, want and expect you to read their minds. And then introverted managers, who expect you to know what they want, become enraged because you have not given them what they think they have asked for. But they have not asked for anything, and that is very frustrating for an extrovert. And it's frustrating for other introverts. Everyone is always on edge. You're always trying to "outguess," always trying to read their thoughts, and you're always sure that you're not going to correctly do it. And in most cases you're right—you don't. Introverts do not make themselves clear. In day-to-day operations, introverts don't even think about the fact that they have not communicated information.

Introverts also don't think about the fact that they are supposed to communicate information. This has been *my* experience. Introverts feel that they have figured it out on their own, so, therefore, everyone else should figure it out on their own, too.

And some introverted managers have no, or little, need for control over their subordinates. Others have more of a need to control. But both cases can be very frustrating to the subordinates.

Elizabeth had different experiences with two introverted managers:

With my first introverted manager, I had to figure out—and it took me a while to do it—that as long as there were no glitches, as long as my manager did not hear anything bad about me, no negative repercussions, as long as we were continuing to meet our targets and build our business, then he really did not need to know anything. He really did not show that he cared, at all, about what we did. I had to figure that out and it took me a while, because I was trying to be a good extroverted subordinate to my introverted boss. After I figured out how much of an introvert he was, I tried to get on his calendar to make reports. But the fact was, he really seemed not to care. Here was an introverted manager without any need for control or aggressive, deliberate management. He left me alone. If I had a problem, and I gave him enough warning, he would be there to help me think it through. But only when I went to him. He never came to me. That was fine with me, but it might not have been fine with either an introvert or even an extrovert who needed some approval. Someone who needed some recognition or affirmation that what they were doing was right. In my case, I got those things from the organization and so I didn't need them from my boss. I did get recognition from him in the form of raises and bonuses, but I never got it in an informal way. Perhaps if an extrovert reporting to an introvert does *not* have a real need for affirmation, then the relationship *can* work very well. But if the extroverted subordinate needs constant feedback, then the relationship can be a disaster.

If you are an extroverted subordinate with an introverted manager and are responsible for the deliverables, this kind of relationship can be damaging. This can really get in the way, especially if delivering all of the extroverted subordinate's writing and creativity to the organization is the responsibility of the introverted manager. And if extroverted subordinates spend weeks putting a program together, only to find that they have been heading off in the wrong direction, increased frustration and problems ensue.

In another situation with another introverted manager, what I learned to do was to just give her anything, which goes against my grain, but at least I would give her something to react to. Once she reacted, I had something to go on. Then I had something to work on, and based on that, I gave her something else, so again, she would react. I had to try to not make it perfect, though, because I had no idea what she really wanted. I just guessed. And she didn't hold it against you if you did not get it. If asked for input and she made an effort to explain, which was never clear, I would put it into writing based on her "fuzzy" direction, but then I'd be in real trouble. It was better to say "here's what I think," and then let her respond to that, knowing that she had not given any input. I think it's better to do a "straw man" (something on your own, not based on feedback from the boss) and get feedback on that rather than get "fuzzy" (or unclear) input up front and then attempt to do something, only to find yourself off the mark. Once something was written down, she had something to bounce off of, and then I was more likely to get clearer feedback. The introverted boss can be terrific at championing the cause, thinking about developing programs, and putting things in place. They'll figure out all of the nuances. But when a team of people has to deliver something based on the vision, and the vision is not clear, the product that you come out with may not be so great. But our team did try to accommodate our boss. We knew her style and we made things work. But it was still very frustrating.

I've known introverts to constantly tinker with things and change things and then neglect to let everyone know how they have tinkered. Introverts like to add on and add on, because everything is a better idea, and then it drowns under its own weight! Everyone is struggling to implement these ideas. It keeps building and building, all of which is brilliant, but everyone else is drowning under all that verbiage. Introverts have a vision, struggle to

communicate it, then want it to be better and better and better.

Introverted managers have a very difficult time
articulating what they want or what needs to be
done. I know people who take other people to
meetings when an introvert is running the meeting
just to have an interpreter figure out what the introvert just said. I hear the words, and it all sounds rea-
sonable, but I come out of the meeting without any
idea of what I'm supposed to do. Giving an introvert something to react to makes life easier. Then
they can react to it, point by point. At least that's
the way I see it.

I asked Michelle, a manager of a business-development
consulting firm and an introvert, whether she views introverts as being mostly assets or liabilities within her company.
"Assets! Of course!" she said. "I think, like all things, there
should be variety and differences, and we need extroverts to
get certain things done, and we need introverts to get other
things done. I definitely feel introverts are an asset." Michelle
continued:

Introverts are more thoughtful. Introverts who
tend to think before they speak are certainly valued. Generally, introverts think about what's happening, about what's going on, and they think about
things more fully. This helps to give *me* time to do
work, because people are not constantly at my door
and in my face constantly talking. It gives me time
to pull away from the fray and accomplish things
that need doing.

I asked Michelle if she could readily tell whether or not an employee is introverted.

I did give the MBTI to one of my staff members when she began working, because I needed someone to counteract my FP [Feeling, Perceiving: one who will spend more time worrying about people's feelings than getting the job done]. I needed someone more extroverted in terms of dealing with clients on the phone. The previous support person was definitely an introvert and that definitely did not work for me in terms of being able to counteract *my* introversion. She was so withdrawn she did not communicate to me what was going on, she didn't close the loop with me, and she was not outgoing with clients. I am an introvert and *I* can still do that. In this case, the introvert was definitely a liability.

On the consultant side, I may pick an extrovert over an introvert in certain situations. With consultants, I tend to look more for general expertise in an area than style. In the financial or the technology area, for example, I would tend to bring in an introvert rather than an extrovert. If I were going to a marketing department or a communications area function, however, I would bring in an extrovert.

And I think my management style would correspond. I think with an introvert, I would have a tendency to micromanage a little bit more, because I don't know what's going on. I'm not getting enough information. I have to "go after" them more. With the extroverts, they come to me. Maybe even more than I want (after all, I'm an introvert). They want to come to me and ask me questions, sit down with me, talk to me, and process things. My overall tendency is to be more hands-off.

The consultants, because they are professionals, know the importance of feedback. They tend to close the loops. In some cases there are probably some introverts that I even trust more than extroverts, because I know they are being more thoughtful about what's going on. The extroverts might just be talking off the top of their heads—appearing to be more "formula" oriented. But, unfortunately, there are some introverts who keep everything to themselves and don't provide feedback. They never tell me anything.

In contrast, Jonathan, another consultant, is a high extrovert. When we go on a marketing call, I open the conversation initially, I say why we are at a particular place, and then sit back and relax, and Jonathan takes over and just talks. He does not gather information, he just talks—which may not always be such a good thing. As I already indicated, I manage both extroverts and introverts, and it feels uncomfortable when I have to do a lot of work—when I've got to be extroverted.

I was on a marketing call recently where the client was introverted, one of my consultants was introverted, and the other consultant was very extroverted. I had to manage it so that the extroverted consultant didn't say anything too soon. We needed more information from the client, and the extroverted consultant was dying to fill in and take over the meeting. I was trying to get the introverted consultant to do more assessing and the client to share more of what he needed. We needed more information in order for me to guide and direct everything. As an introverted manager, I was not enjoying having to manage and direct everything. It was very hard for me. It was a struggle.

Following the meeting, we did have a debriefing session, though. "Here are some of the problems as I perceive them, and here's where we need to be moving forward," I said. "We need to manage these kinds of situations better." The introvert was not surprised by the debriefing, although I think she did some weird things in that meeting like asking questions but never explaining to the client why she was asking these questions; she was just gathering data. Where the extrovert wasn't gathering *any* data. He was just listening to the sound of his own voice. He wanted to get on his platform and start selling. Of course, he's a sales trainer as well, so it makes sense. He's very geared toward his extroversion. He was very clear as to what was going on at this meeting. My introverted consultant-team member was a little oblivious to it. She kept blaming the client for not being forthcoming. She was surprised by the feedback that *her* style was not forthcoming in this meeting. But she found the feedback helpful and appreciated it.

It's important to help introverts further develop professionally in the workplace. Give them training, especially presentation-skills training and sales training. Give concrete hands-on models and behavior-modification techniques to teach behaviors that "look" extroverted, to allow them to work in a more extroverted world.

Michelle's tips align with the objectives, goals, and techniques presented in this book. And they speak to much of my inspiration and ideas for writing it. She goes on to demonstrate ways that managers can help introverts to be assets in their company:

> Put introverts in important roles that are visible. Allow them to show their strengths rather than harp on their weaknesses. Encourage introverts to contribute to their company's research department. They need to let people know what a valuable asset they are to the company, which is why we began having them write the weekly newsletter. It reminds people that they are around, and of the valuable work that they do.
>
> As I said earlier, introverts are great thinkers. So, people who do career and personality assessments are great assets to the company and the clients. Assessments need to be thoughtful, rather than have a lot of pizzazz. And looking at other strengths, introverts make good trainers also, because introverted trainers are more sensitive to the introverted participants and can draw them out in a classroom setting. Extroverted trainers don't even notice the introverts in the room, and they intimidate the introverts.

Michelle has always worked as an independent consultant. She started her own business with two partners five years ago, and it has grown into a multimillion-dollar firm. One partner has since retired; Michelle's other partner is a very high extrovert.

> My partner, Shelley, and I have the most tension around my introversion and her extroversion. She is

really the marketing person. She always wants to debrief, and process everything that has gone on, and talk and talk. Shelley thinks that she is an introvert, but in reality she really is an exhausted extrovert. There is no way she could do what she does and be an introvert. She expects me to be more extroverted, and I'm sure I expect her to be more introverted. She wants to talk about everything, she wants to process everything, she wants to mull over things with me; I can talk about it for five seconds and I'm done. I can leave a message on her voicemail and I'm done. She'll never use E-mail. She prefers to talk. I like E-mail because it's quiet and I can write. Shelley likes to talk, but both Shelley and I have our strengths, our assets, *and* our place in business.

At the beginning of this book, I cited material from an article by Carducci and Zimbardo in *Psychology Today* titled "Shy?" The article gave some pointers on helping others to beat shyness, and stated that because one out of two people surveyed were considered shy, we should be sensitive to the fact that some people may not be as outgoing or confident as others. It is the job of managers, especially, to make their staff comfortable. Even introverted managers should consciously try to bring out the best in others.

One manager stated earlier that she had a problem in assuming that people knew what she was thinking about, when they really did not have a clue. The manager admitted to having temper tantrums because her needs had not been met. In this case, the manager said she is learning to communicate more clearly with her staff. And this is a sign of heightened awareness. Introverts and extroverts, managers and friends, and family members and business associates should all demonstrate respect, greater sensitivity, and increased awareness and understanding of introverts.

Many managers in this chapter have discussed personality types and their interrelationships. I suggest you visit a qualified career consultant and take the Myers-Briggs Type Indicator yourself to find out what *your* "type" is. It helps with managing our job relationships, and points to breakdowns in our communications with others. But, in addition to that, learning some general concepts about and applications of personality types will give you new insight about the nature and behavior of people. This helps foster better communication. And taking the MBTI with a consultant will help you improve your direction and the management of your own all-encompassing lifestyle. And besides, taking it is fun!

I've borrowed a small sample of work from a wonderful book called *The Personality Type Tool Kit* (1995) by Paul D. Tieger and Barbara Barron-Tieger.* They are the authors of *Do What You Are* (1992), another extraordinarily helpful book. Sharing the insights presented in the heavily researched *Tool Kit*, I will focus on the details of my "type." I am an INTP (Introvert, Intuitive, Thinking, Perceiving), and there are not many of us around. We actually represent less than 1 percent of the population. The INTP weakness that struck me most in the *Tool Kit* was the tendency to "be impatient with and critical of people less competent than I." Now, I did not really want to hear that, but I know I really do have a tendency to lose patience with people that I perceive "just don't get it"— whatever the "it" is.

I will also discuss the strengths and weaknesses of a few other types. The sixteen types are also profiled in the chart in the beginning of this chapter. (Additional resources are listed in the Resources section.)

---

*Information on pages 109–114 reprinted from *The Personality Type Tool Kit* with permission from the authors. All rights reserved.

INTP
Introvert, Intuitive, Thinking, Perceiving

INTPS represent approximately 1 percent of the American population.

What I Need in a Career for It to Be Satisfying

1. The ability to concentrate on one creative challenge at a time, giving it my full attention without a lot of interruptions

2. The opportunity to develop innovative approaches and systems but not get bogged down in the details of implementation

3. An atmosphere of professionalism and mutual respect, where my expertise is recognized and respected and I have some say in how I am evaluated and compensated

4. An unstructured environment that encourages free thinking and improvisation, without senseless rules, unnecessary meetings, or paperwork

5. The chance to logically analyze existing and potential systems and make recommendations for strategically sound changes

Careers to Consider

- Computer software designer
- Research/development specialist
- New market/product designer
- Psychologist/psychoanalyst
- Financial analyst
- Archaeologist
- College professor
- Inventor
- Creative writer
- Entertainer/dancer
- Computer programmer
- Database manager
- Scientist: chemistry
- Scientist: biology
- Mathematician
- Photographer

continued on next page

- Agent
- Researcher
- Economist
- Lawyer
- Investigator
- Musician
- Systems analyst
- Strategic planner
- Neurologist
- Physicist
- Plastic surgeon
- Pharmacist
- Architect
- Historian
- Philosopher
- Logician
- Artist

Recommendations for the Job Search

A. Capitalizing on My Strengths

   1. Use my long-range vision to anticipate future career needs

   2. Create my own career or modify available jobs to be more satisfying

   3. Communicate my intelligence and competence to interviewers

   4. Be innovative when designing my job search plan and creative in getting interviews

   5. Weigh the pros and cons of choices and keep my options open

B. Avoiding My Weaknesses

   1. Establish and stick to a plan of action

   2. Pay attention to important details and facts

3. Follow through on all phases of the search, including the "niceties"

4. Generate and communicate energy and enthusiasm during interviews

5. Make decisions along the way to avoid missing better opportunities

INTP Strengths

- Using creativity and insight to understand issues in depth

- Applying logical analysis to complex problems

- Working alone with great focus and concentration

- Learning new skills and technology with ease and competence

- Engaging in long range and strategic thinking

INTP Weaknesses

- Acting impatient with and critical of people less competent than I

- Developing such complicated arguments or ideas that no one else understands them

- Considering only the possible implications, rather than the realistic applications of my ideas

- Refusing to deal with repetitious or mundane projects

- Intimidating others by my independent and confident style

ISTJ
Introvert, Sensing, Thinking, Judging

ISTJS represent approximately 6 percent of the American population.

ISTJ Strengths

- Following and adhering to established routines and procedures

- Working alone without being supervised or needing to socialize

- Handling situations of high pressure and stress with calmness

- Completing all parts of my work with accuracy and precision

- Remembering the important details of projects and not letting them fall through the cracks

ISTJ Weaknesses

- Avoiding different ways of doing things or untested approaches

- Discouraging dissension or resisting change

- Making snap decisions without consulting other people

- Being impatient with inefficient people or systems

- Forgetting to offer compliments or to express my appreciation of others

ISFJ
Introvert, Sensing, Feeling, Judging

ISFJs represent approximately 6 percent of the American population.

ISFJ Strengths

- Working hard, doing whatever is needed until the job is finished

- Respecting the chain of command and following necessary rules and procedures

- Helping others by explaining tasks with patience and clarity

- Working with routines or repeated, sequential tasks

- Carefully and thoroughly dealing with details and documenting activities

ISFJ Weaknesses

- Not addressing conflict and not asserting needs

- Resisting new or unconventional methods

- Getting immersed in the details of work and not seeing the big picture

- Becoming overwhelmed when several projects need attention at once

- Becoming discouraged when not feeling appreciated or needed

ENFP
Extrovert, Intuitive, Feeling, Perceiving

ENFPs represent approximately 5 percent of the American population.

ENFP Strengths

- Seeing unique ways of solving problems

- Working with all kinds of people as part of a team

- Applying various experiences and skills to new fields of interest

- Understanding other people and getting them excited about ideas

- Being flexible, accommodating, and easy to work with

ENFP Weaknesses

- Getting sidetracked or becoming distracted by something more interesting

- Not preparing properly ahead of time

- Becoming bored or disinterested when working alone

- Being sloppy with details or facts

It's really eye-opening to learn more about yourself and your personality type. And, as you'll see later, the job search consists of only three components for you to contemplate:

1. Who am I?

2. Where do I want to go?

3. How am I going to get there?

Now let's examine a few more "managing the introvert" situations. Stacey, the assistant program manager, presents another management style.

An introvert, Stacey reported to an introvert in her last position (when I first met her), but Stacey never really knew what her introverted manager thought or what she wanted.

> I had to just get a sense or a feel, because being an introvert, for me, also means I don't want to hurt someone's feelings by criticizing them, and I think my manager didn't particularly like to be critical either. When things went wrong there was tension and things went unsaid. She would give me looks across the room, so I knew something was wrong, but I didn't know what. And I didn't ask. So things remained unspoken. She wasn't clear. She had it in her head, but wasn't clear about direction, and I, being an introvert, wasn't going back to ask for direction, because I felt I was supposed to know. So in some cases it was like the "blind leading the blind." It had to get to the point where we were both just so uncomfortable, that finally she blew up. Which was bad. It would reach the point where she was shouting. "You did this wrong, you did that wrong" . . . on and on. So now, unfortunately, there were criticisms and hurt feelings.
>
> When it comes to *my* managerial style, I'm OK when I don't encounter fools. I can't tolerate people who don't have common sense. I see it as self-preservation, which will force me to do the right thing. Therefore, I will force myself to try to manage situations by telling my direct report where the

problems are. I learned from the way I had been managed—or *not* managed. I try to be clear in terms of what I want. I even give examples. Friends, family, everybody will get the same from me. But don't ask me questions you already know the answers to.

"Introverts are seen as liabilities in my company," says Nat, a comptroller of a real estate firm, who is working toward becoming a financial planner.

Yet it is we introverts who are keeping this company attached to reality. However, we don't get rewarded. In fact, extroverted management plays the game of "shoot the messenger." I truly believe it is the extroverts who are going to bring this company to its knees. When I arrived, the company was verging on bankruptcy, and the extroverts were out looking for million-dollar deals. But when you run the numbers, they've also lost over a million dollars doing the deal.

I manage both introverts and extroverts the same. The most important thing in managing is communication. Now, I know I would have to force additional communication when managing an introvert. For me, when managing an extrovert, the communication is easier.

Christopher, a science professor, has increasingly assumed management responsibilities at his university:

I am an introvert in an introverted setting, in the world of academia. Academia is a research environment, which makes it a well-chosen field for me. However, over the years, I have had to pull an increasing load as an administrator. And as a result of my prominence as a scientist, I have been put on scientist-administration committees in Washington, D.C. I have to go to Washington to meet with complete strangers from other fields and attempt to convince them that one or another project is important. That is a kind of moral weight that is placed on me that is very uncomfortable, because although I have an arrogant conviction about what I want to do, that does not extend to the choices that I make for others. I have to make decisions on where the field moves, but I want others to make their own choices about where they want to go and what they want to do. I don't want to have control of others. It's a weird situation for me to be in. I would much rather lead by example than by direction.

As a result of that, I wound up being chair of my department. And this is not something that is easy for me because I'm now responsible for hiring, firing, and evaluating the faculty. I'm responsible for making sure that all the special events occur on the right day, at the right time, and with the right menu! I'm responsible for the menus! It involves lots of interactions with large numbers of people in the corporation. When I have to call them, that means that they are also calling me, and that is very difficult. Usually, what I want to do is get right back to doing my thing.

As an introverted manager, I have a reputation for occasional acts of temper displays—and I know where it comes from. I like the people I supervise to show initiative. If I feel they are coming back to me for reassurance, *that* makes me unhappy. I like them to report in with the end result. I don't like them to treat me like an air-traffic controller. Because of this, some people have pursued a false strategy, and the corrections cannot be made until later. I am not the volunteer fire department and I have trained them not to sound the alarm unless there is smoke coming out of the building. That means that they wind up far more exposed than they might be if they had a boss who micromanaged. They give me a schedule, I approve it, they go and do it. That's the way I manage. I want you to go and make your own decision, but the organizational liability that I have is that that decision may blow up. I've tried to solve this problem by making sure that everyone who works for me is smart and funny, or at least able to laugh it off. I wind up with these good people who work for me, so I then have to set aside my disposition toward tempers and remember to lead with goodwill. This is something else that's been very difficult for me, but I now feel I am capable of providing reassurance along the way. The funny thing is, one of my old assistants told me that I was never more menacing than when I was aiming to be reassuring.

I told Christopher, "As an introvert I have a difficult time asking for direction. For example, I will need help from you but I don't want you to yell at me, because then I will be crushed. If I were an extrovert, I might be more inclined to laugh off your attack, but as an introvert, that could be hard for me."

Yes, and that is the catch-22. I have to make sure that there is a certain level of confidence up front. Then everything else can really be worked out. When I realize that I have made a mistake, I have to be willing to make the correction. I may not be able to make the correction as impetuously as I want to, but I can live with that. I've had introverts working for me, and they have had the most difficult time with my style. But they have taught me. The introverts were the ones I was able to learn from when I knew I had this way of interacting with them that would keep things functioning at a very high level.

In a scientific lab, there has to be a very high level of trust. You must trust the people taking the measures. I thought, if I set the technique bar very high, I would get people with whom I would be confident, but of course confidence is not just about how well and how carefully you measure. It's about how responsible you are as an individual. You have to court somebody and win their confidence. It has nothing to do with proficiency. It has to do with trust. In order for me, an introvert, to establish trust with an introvert, I really had to put the time in, be patient and do the necessary self-sacrificing to make sure that it would work. And then, of course, it works better, and they become fanatically devoted.

I learned my lesson, but I could not have done it without some coaching. My coach was constantly advising me on how to behave in the workplace. My coach/tutor counseled me for two years on how to work this through. Coaching was difficult for both of us because of my arrogance and my "I know how to do this" attitude. I had incorrectly identified it as a technical problem. And that was a matter of naïveté and arrogant confidence.

Based on what the managers in this chapter have revealed about how they manage introverts, I created the "Managing for Results" chart detailing the actions that can be taken and the results possible when a manager perceives that a communication problem is attributable to introversion.

Managing for Results

Manager Observes a Challenge

Employee has lots of answers but does not speak up in meetings

Employee's Present Behavior

Sometimes appears withdrawn; is perceived by others as arrogant, aloof, and a non–team player

Manager's Input

Reach out and have regular conversations with employee
Be encouraging
In a private conversation, say how much you value employee's input and sharing of ideas
Talk about employee's needs and your needs as a manager
Send employee to a seminar that focuses on communication skills for introverts

Recognized Result for Employee

Feels valued and appreciated
Becomes a team player
Self-esteem and confidence increases
Communicates more freely and begins to establish rapport
Receives greater respect and is considered for a promotion

It should be clear how valuable it can be to understand the many ways in which people can be classified. And whether we're managers or staffers, introverts or extroverts, or some of both, we should recognize that people are different.

Everyone has a different style of communication; even within the categories of introversion and extroversion there are forms of communication that some people respond to better than others. For example, some people are most comfortable with hands-on training while others prefer explanation. While *you* may just want the facts, your coworker may want to develop a sense of relationship before you start swapping statistics. So take time to ask questions, listen, and observe, so that you can identify other people's needs.

Many forms of behavior that indicate introversion were revealed by these interviews. Both managers and employees should become aware of these behaviors so they can identify when their conflicts are being caused by a clash between introverted and extroverted ways of communicating. Have you ever heard your coworkers complain that their opinions are being ignored, or that people think they aren't interested enough to offer opinions? Have you ever been accused of not offering enough information or of not being outgoing enough with clients? These sentiments are often red flags that introversion is at the heart of the problem. Whether you're an introverted employee, a manager of introverted employees, or an introverted manager yourself, recognizing that these situations can be resolved by understanding the difference in how introverts and extroverts communicate is essential to establishing more fluid lines of communication. As one manager said, both introverts and extroverts are needed for a smoothly operating business, and "communication is a vital link."

7

COMMUNICATION

"Always go to other people's funerals, otherwise they won't come to yours."

YOGI BERRA

Stanford Business School professor Thomas Harrell gathered the records of Stanford Business School graduates and noted that verbal fluency is the most significant predictor of a person's success. "The verbally fluent are able to sell themselves, their services and their companies—all critical skills for running a corporation. Shy (or introverted) people are probably those behind the scenes designing the cars, programs and computers. And these are very impressive feats, but they don't pay as much as CEO," (Carducci and Zimbardo 1995).

A lot of the discussion in previous chapters relates to how people communicate and listen to one another. Our communication styles—how we hear, pay attention, and give feedback—are key to success in our lives. Therefore it's important to have strong communication skills and effective listening skills.

Both shy and introverted people are often gifted listeners. During a conversation, they often pay extremely close attention to the person speaking—but have problems when it's expected that they briskly respond back. It's important to show other people that you are interested in them and what they have to say.

Active listening is needed to effectively communicate. While listening, look interested in the speaker and periodically paraphrase what you hear them say. Listen for emotional undertones and return *your* comments with similar emotional reinforcement. Intermittently injecting phrases such as "uh huh" or "really!" tell the speaker that you are following their ideas. These words encourage the speaker to continue the conversation. The more engaging your conversation, the greater your chance of garnering information and/or satisfying your request.

This active listening can take you from passive to active communication. And *active* communication can lead you to an informational meeting or even to the job interview that you seek.

As I've said before, introverts may already *have* the conversational skills and self-esteem needed to interact with others, but prefer to be alone. Shy people want very much to be with other people but lack the necessary social skills, self-confidence, and self-esteem.

When I asked Portia (the former director of a women's philanthropic not-for-profit organization) whether she had ever knowingly experienced communication drawbacks or felt that introverts could not be at the top, she emphatically answered, "No, not at all." Portia thinks, in fact, that she excelled in leadership roles. But she was always exhausted and didn't understand why. Now she understands more about her type, as spelled out for her in the MBTI, and it seems, she explained, that she was trying to function on two levels:

> I was trying to do all of this processing as an introvert, internally, but then always had to do heavy

external communication, which was, for me, an extra effort. But I'm sure it comes naturally to an extrovert. I feel I had to do more work, though, than extroverts do, when it comes to communication in an extroverted environment. In retrospect, I remember having communication problems growing up. I'm very much like my dad, who is an introvert also. We would try to communicate with each other but experienced difficulty, because we were both such internal processors that it was hard to get outside of our heads to talk to each other.

By now it should be pretty clear that introverts are not great communicators. Besides being out of the loop when it comes to this vital, everyday skill, when introverts tend to avoid building rapport with coworkers and their managers, and don't make an effort to stay closely connected, problems rapidly develop. Often, the compounded danger for introverts lies in how extroverts perceive them.

Joanne came to me for executive coaching after being fired from a not-for-profit organization. She had originally been hired as the assistant director, then rose to become the executive director, a position she held for twelve years. When she arrived at the organization, it had $400,000 in the bank. On the day she was asked to leave, the account contained over $3 million. Joanne had taken over a dysfunctional, divided staff and turned it into a solid team. She had constructed several programs around community outreach. Higher-level officials in both the city and state governments knew and respected her. She served on several corporate boards. Yet her own board asked Joanne to leave, claiming they had lost confidence in her.

What happened? How did it happen?

Despite the pain she felt, and the litigation she was involved in, Joanne knew she had to move forward to find a new position. As is standard in the search process, my staff and I began with an assessment of Joanne's skills, including her personality type. It soon became clear that she was an introvert.

When Joanne received a call from an executive recruiter for a position in another city as a director of a nationwide, low-cost housing company, she panicked. What was she going to say about the reason for leaving her previous position? She had been vague even with me, her counselor, whom she trusted. It gradually became clear that the underlying reason for the dismissal was "lack of communication." Well, Joanne reasoned, if her original board had a problem with her ability to communicate, why would another board want to hire her, when getting ideas across was so vital to someone at the directorship level?

We went back and forth on this issue, finally deciding to go to "the street" for information. Not-for-profit companies have a vast gossip network. Maybe we could find out what the official word was out there. Joanne approached other executive directors, who we assumed would have the inside story. And guess what we found out? *Nothing.* Everyone agreed that they'd heard nothing negative about Joanne: She had not absconded with funds; she had not harassed employees; and the board still respected her. So why exactly was she fired?

Joanne came up with three reasons: To begin with, the previous year, due to budget cuts in Washington, she had lost funding for a summer day-care program, and tried to fix it without notifying the board that the funds had been cut. During that same fiscal year she lost a teen program. Then she replaced her assistant with someone not of the board's choosing.

To outsiders, any one of these may appear to be relatively minor issues, and easily fixable. In fact, when the board found out about the day-care program, they were angry essentially because if they had known, they would have funded it from other sources. But Joanne felt like a failure. It was *her* job to see that these programs happened. The more funds were cut, the more noncommunicative she became with her board. She could not ask for their help. They had hired her to do a job, and she was going to do it! Except it was becoming increasingly impossible for her to function without enlisting the board's help. Matters deteriorated rapidly, until, in fact, there *was* a serious communication problem. The board did lose confidence in her. Joanne's response was to become even more introverted, and she lost her job.

The situation was so painful, she couldn't explain it. By the time she flew to Boston for her third interview, the executive recruiter was apoplectic. He feared the truth involved a horrible mess—or why wouldn't Joanne discuss it?

Unhappily, Joanne's story is not uncommon. But with coaching and the unclouding of issues, she was retained by the new board for a year, on a consulting basis. It is not a perfect happy ending, but it is an ending that is better than most.

Communication is key to organizational leadership and when there is a breakdown in communication, trouble looms on the horizon. No manager likes surprises. Joanne didn't ask for help when information and help was needed. She didn't network. And learning how to effectively communicate and effectively network is a process.

Remember the "good old days" when we worked sane hours? Nine-to-five was defined as a full-time job. Well, no more. In today's busy, hectic world, many people are still in the office at 10 and 11 P.M. For many introverts, these schedules are acceptable because they offer peace and quiet in the office. Many introverts get their best ideas when there is room to roam in their heads, rehash the questions on various issues, and come up with solutions.

In an extroverted organizational environment, people want immediate answers to their questions. As an introvert, however, an "instantaneous" answer may really not be the best solution. Therefore, the phrase, "I need to think about this and get back to you," should become one of your most important responses. Trust me on this one. Instantaneous decision making is not the introvert's strength. No one is good at everything. Introverts need to think about all the alternatives, weigh all the pros and cons, then get back with the right decision, rather than one that is not well considered.

Many introverts enjoy the peace and quiet of having time to themselves. They find their private time too easily invaded and tend to adapt by developing a high power of concentration that can shut out nearby conversations, ringing telephones, and the like.

Many programmers and systems analysts have this high power of concentration, able to exclude everything around them. The stereotypical programmer sits in front of a monitor for hours, while the outside world goes about its daily business. The level of concentration is so intense, the programmer may only get up for an occasional soda or to use the rest room. Some programmers have taken introversion to an incredible intensity, and indeed lack the social skills necessary for interaction with the rest of us earthly beings. This is introversion of the highest order, and may be a little neurotic as well, but it does show how some introverts can live in their own worlds and only come out when they want to.

Often introverts are perceived as being "great listeners" but feel that others take advantage of them. Introverts can sit in a meeting and appear to be uninvolved. While the extroverts are arguing, trying to get their points across, the introvert is in the corner (our favorite spot) seemingly paying no attention. However, at the meeting's end, it will usually be the introvert who summarizes and pulls the meeting together. As the extroverts are talking over and around each other, the introverts are making sense of the proceedings.

Most introverts have been called "shy" from time to time. They are perceived by others as somewhat reserved and reflective. And introverts get a bum rap. The perception is that introverts are distant or arrogant. Although this may or may not be true, many people interpret their perceptions as reality. Is the introvert quietly paying attention, or is he or she quietly thinking everyone is an idiot?

Introverts also like to share special occasions with just one other person or perhaps a few close friends. The two biggest obstacles facing the hundreds of introverts with whom I have worked over several years are their shared inability to (1) talk on the phone, especially with a stranger, and (2) enjoy a large party. An introvert will arrive at a party and gravitate to the kitchen with one or two people rather than stay in the living room engaging in conversation with large groups. Or they latch on to the periphery of a large living-room group, hover around the third-point line, and do not contribute anything to the conversation. That way, they can appear to be part of the group without conversing with anyone. The problem is that no one really knows who they are. At a work-related function, the introvert could be missing out on some very vital information. And social occasions offer valuable opportunities for networking.

One of the consultants with whom I collaborate was invited to a very big Fourth of July celebration on Martha's Vineyard. All the movers and shakers of the universe were there. While she was sitting in the corner of the deck, conversing about something innocuous, everyone else was exchanging cards. No one even watched the fireworks. They were too busy arranging meetings. By the end of the party, millions of dollars in business deals had taken place, but the only information my colleague learned about was the best beach for her children on the island! If you're helping to run a business, you need to think, behave, and communicate like the rest of the extroverted masters of the universe. My colleague missed an important opportunity, which she vows never to repeat.

Most introverts wish they could express their ideas more forcefully; they resent those who blurt out things they were just about to say. "I woulda, coulda, shoulda" become very familiar words after the fact, right? "If only I had talked about the Johnson account!" Introverts do need to think in order to talk. It's true. But there are times when we really do know a topic better than others and we just freeze. To function more in the unfrozen zone, take a deep breath and count to ten, as simple as this sounds. First silently rehearse, and then go ahead and speak. Make sure you are presenting enough data to back up your thoughts.

Introverts like stating their thoughts or feelings without interruptions; they allow others to speak in the hope that they will reciprocate when it comes time for them to speak. When you feel you are constantly being interrupted, you must take control. There is nothing wrong with a simple but direct "please let me finish." If the person interrupting you continues to ignore your request, they will begin to look boorish and rude. Better that, than that you come across as mild and meek.

Reneé, an M.B.A. banker, is an introvert who deliberately sets out to conquer her natural, preferred tendency to interact only one-on-one.

> I've gotten to be pretty good at talking to strangers on the train. I know this is not an introverted tendency, but I live in New Jersey and commute into New York, so there's lots of time on the train to try and connect with a stranger. So I start conversations with complete strangers on the commuter train, on the way into the city.

What I look for are people who pull out magazines, preferably two or more, one of which is hopefully in one of the fields that my business is in. I can then start a conversation with that as a lead-in, using their prompts—the magazines. I can start from there, they hear genuine interest, it's one-on-one, and there is an artificial time constraint because the train will pull in at a specific time. The time I spend with this total stranger is about the same time as an informational interview (about twenty-five minutes). And it's great practice for the informational interview. There's really nothing to lose, and everything to gain. There is absolutely no downside risk. At the same time, I have a captive audience. They're not going anywhere, they *can't* go anywhere.

When Reneé approaches someone and finds they really don't want to talk, though, she'll drop it. And she finds men much more approachable than women. "Few things work better than the *Wall Street Journal* or the *New York Times*. And I do get leads," she adds. "It's a great technique."

Indeed, it sounds like Reneé has come up with a wonderful technique to practice her networking.

Communication is the key to networking. Introverts must accept their natural tendency to keep things to themselves and find ways to compensate for it. Learn to take advantage of important opportunities at social events: cultivate your natural tendency toward listening, take the time you need to respond, and demand (politely) that you be heard. All this takes practice, but if, like Reneé, you are willing to look for such practice opportunities in your everyday life, you will realize your goal of achieving successful communication and thus, successful networking.

Networking Exercises

"If you come to a fork in the road, take it."
Yogi Berra

When Julia said she realized that her career change was a process, she also meant that she spent quite a lot of time completing assessment exercises—like those included in this chapter. This chapter also reviews the networking process.

What Is Networking?

Networking is the process of asking people you know (or could get to know through others) for information, advice, ideas, or moral support as you plan and pursue your career goals.

A networking strategy involves two phases:

1. Identifying the appropriate people to contact

2. Speaking with these people in person to gather the assistance you desire

Networking is the most effective job-search technique you can employ. The reason is simple: managers want to hire individuals whom they know, from their own experience, are good workers or people for whom others will vouch. The smartest way to conduct a job search is to work closely with your human resource manager and to take charge yourself with a well-planned networking strategy.

Networking, by definition, does not guarantee results. It must be done well—in a way that works for you and also within the culture of your organization. Your networking efforts must be direct, focused, and not wasteful of others' time. You must make it *easy* for your contacts to help you.

What Is a Contact

A contact is a person with whom you can speak about your career goals and who may be able to direct you to other individuals who can do the same. There are two kinds of contacts: primary and secondary. Primary contacts are people you know (a former boss, coworkers, and so on). They are the first step in setting up a network but are not usually the people who can hire you. Primary contacts can lead you to secondary contacts. Secondary contacts are people who may be in a position to know of openings and maybe even hire you. Start with primary contacts and branch out, with their help, to secondary contacts. Secondary contacts are willing to meet you because you are no longer a stranger, but, through your primary contact's referrals, a "known quantity."

Examples of Contacts

The best contacts often come from your workplace, including your current and former managers, human resource managers, and your coworkers and former coworkers. You may also have acquaintances (in sports, the PTA, social and business clubs, church, and so on) who work for a firm or field in which you're interested, or who know others who do. Your fellow college or professional-school alumni also make ideal contacts, because they most likely share your interests and experience. Even consultants or vendors who work with a firm in which you are interested are good contacts, because they often work with a variety of groups and managers.

Goals of the Networking Process

You should use networking for several purposes. First, networking enables you to obtain information about an area, function, division, or group in which you are interested but are unsure whether, or how, you might fit in. Obtaining advice from or brainstorming with a respected and knowledgeable individual about your next job move is another networking goal. Finally, networking lets others know of your availability and enlists their help in referring you to potential hiring managers when they learn of opportunities.

Networking Dos and Don'ts

Dos	Don'ts
• Do your homework before you meet with a contact and ask questions. Research his or her area, function, or product through internal brochures, the Internet, business periodicals, or others whom you know. • Do meet with your contact in person, especially if you do not already know the person. Telephone	• Don't ask for a job. Don't expect your network to function as a placement office. • Don't ask someone to send your resume around. • Don't expect too much too soon. It can take time for network "seeds" to grow. • Don't assume others know your background, even if they know you well.

continued on next page

Networking Dos and Don'ts

Dos	Don'ts
"meetings" are seldom productive.	• Don't break confidentiality regarding the activities of your current organization.
• Do prepare an agenda in advance—know why you're meeting with this person, how he or she can help you, and what advice you seek. Prepare your thoughts, ideas, and questions. Give a brief overview (your two-minute pitch) of your background and career goals.	• Don't give the impression that you're looking for "any old job" by not having a focus or being all things to all people.
• Do educate your contacts to work for you by explaining what you do, what you are looking for, and how they can help you. Be specific and concise.	• Don't be discouraged if someone brushes you off. Don't take it personally—it will happen in very fast-paced environments. Try someone else.
• Do keep expanding your network. Ask each contact for an additional name or two of someone else with whom you could talk: "Can you suggest anyone else I might talk to about this?"	• Don't bend the truth. If your position is in the process of being downsized, say so. Work with a career counselor to develop, as part of your pitch, the reason why you are looking for a new position. Don't pretend you're doing idle research.
• Do try to reciprocate as often as possible. Try to give as much as you	• Don't forget to send a thank-you note to your contact if he or she was helpful.

continued on next page

Networking Dos and Don'ts

Dos	Don'ts
receive from your network. The more people you help, the more will help you.	• Don't forget to inform anyone who gives you a lead about the outcome.
• Do practice before you begin. Review how you are going to present yourself. Role-play with someone you trust or a friend familiar with the firm in which you're interested.	• Don't arrange meetings only at your convenience or disregard your contact's preferences and schedule.
• Do keep the door open for follow-up with your contact.	
• Do view the networking process as one that will provide a safe climate in which you can try out your ideas before you risk them in a job interview.	

The following contact checklist will help you think of people you know or may have forgotten about. You should try to constantly expand and revise your list of contacts.

Contact List "Memory Jogger"

The Workplace

_____ Your current manager

continued on next page

_____ Your human resource manager

_____ Former managers

_____ Coworkers and former coworkers

_____ Social acquaintances (sports, PTA, social and business clubs, church, and so on) who also work with you

_____ Fellow college or professional-school alumni who work with you

_____ Business acquaintances (review your Rolodex)

_____ Fellow professionals in your field (see membership lists)

_____ Members of your professional societies

_____ People you've met at conventions

_____ Speakers at meetings you've attended

_____ Trade-association executives

_____ Chamber of Commerce

Outside the Workplace

_____ Manager of the branch where you bank

_____ Friends

_____ Social acquaintances

_____ Classmates and fellow alumni

_____ Service professionals: doctors, dentists, opticians, thera-pists, lawyers, accountants, real estate agents, insurance agents, brokers, travel agents, hairdressers, bartenders

_____ Politicians: local, state, and national office holders; political party members

_____ Teachers: your college professors; your children's teachers

_____ Relatives

Preparing for the Information Interview

Remember: The person you are meeting does not know why you are there. *You* have requested time with them. They have graciously accepted. You now need to use this time to your advantage:

- Know *why* you are meeting this person (for example, a friend told you this person is very influential in the field in which you are interested).

- Define the specific *purpose* of the meeting.

- Prepare three to five questions before the meeting.

- Rehearse a two-minute pitch to explain your background. (For more information about the two-minute pitch, see Chapter 10, pages 184–190.)

- Research the background and company for whom this person works.

Structure of the Information Interview

Although each meeting will vary, the following steps offer basic guidelines for the structure of the information interview:

1. Break the ice by discussing your mutual friend or acquaintance.

2. Explain specifically why you wanted to speak to this person.

3. Describe your background (your two-minute pitch, to offer context for your questions).

4. Ask questions about the job function, industry, or company.

- Prepare three to five open-ended questions in advance about which the other party would have insights.

- Probe for more information in a conversational way.

- Pick up on what he or she is saying to discover the needs in the company or industry.

- Ask about good recruiters in your field and the salary you might earn.

- Listen for names of people for whom you could later ask for a referral.

- Watch for ways you could reciprocate.

- Conversationally mention your achievements or experience if appropriate.

5. Ask for referrals.

6. Gather more information regarding referrals.

7. Close the meeting.

- Give thanks.

- Discuss the next step concerning referrals.

- Say that you would like to stay in touch.

8. Write a thank-you note and follow up.

Control of the meeting is yours at the beginning—always—because you initiated it. The control should shift to the other party only if he or she sees you as a candidate for a position within the unit or company. You can tell the shift is happening when suddenly you are being asked the questions instead of asking them. Remember that this is not a job interview. If you don't get the opportunity to elaborate upon your background, that's fine.

Finally, remember that follow-up is the key to success.

Strive to learn something useful for your search, and get referrals unless the meeting has turned into a job interview.

When you've reached this point in the networking process, you'll realize that finding the job that reflects your passion and skills takes preparation, practice, and action. You're on the path toward change, and the interview for that perfect job is probably just around the next bend.

9

NETWORK MANAGEMENT

"Nobody goes there anymore. It's too crowded."
YOGI BERRA

The "Networking for Introverts" Workshop

Years ago, when I started the planning for my Networking for Introverts seminar, I had to present the idea to a bunch of extroverts. "Not fair!" they attacked. "It's discriminatory! We'll picket outside of the conference room!" Then, one fairly sane extrovert said, "Oh, leave them alone. Introverts need somewhere to go to get away from us extroverts." Besides, the group concluded, I would look pretty stupid because introverts would come and no one would talk for two hours.

Well, that was the beginning of an era. Introverts did come. And so did shy extroverts, who were having trouble networking as well. The seminar grew, and the rest is history. But if I had not stood my ground in that initial meeting, I would not have had the opportunity to write this book.

At one of my recent workshops, I recorded some of the responses of some of the participants. Rhonda, who works as a marketing executive in financial services, told the group that when she's involved in her passion, things flow quite naturally and nicely. Rhonda is slightly extroverted, but she's really a borderline introvert. Rhonda, in fact, is an introverted leader and likes to talk and share.

Rhonda shared with us that she regularly incorporates certain energizing lifestyle techniques into her life. They include meditation and yoga. But she also blushingly admitted that she builds in a time to be still—literally—as she delightfully sits quietly within the breathtaking confines of . . . the bathroom stall—*at work!*

Portia also talked about her need to build in "alone time":

> During the day, I deliberately think about activities that I can do that will refresh me, as I free myself from distractions. A good one is closing my door and writing. Or I read a particular author whose work I can get absorbed in. This is great for me. That absorption can be really refreshing! Afterwards, I can then get on with the "group" work. So, now I deliberately identify times for just working internally. And it really helps me manage myself better.

Some of the other workshop participants included an accountant, a marketing product developer, and a special events person—who, like the others, is an introvert, but she was working in an extremely extroverted cable entertainment company. Lori, another participant, told us that at her job, she was considered mousy, and not outgoing enough. And Linda commented that she is more concerned with quality although most companies and extroverts are not, though they insist otherwise. "The extroverts say they are committed to excellence, but they are really not," echoed the others. And they all seemed to agree that when it comes to organizational structure, "it's all a game." One woman told us that she is a modest type of person and does not toot her own horn. She gives the credit at work to her team instead of to herself, which we know can work against her, if she is not careful.

Scenarios, Scripts, and Other Tips

Hands-on experience, practice assignments, and actual scripts can help introverts with the following networking techniques:

- How to get past the "gatekeeper" (usually the administrative assistant)

- What to say first

- How to lead and direct a conversation

- Key questions, gambits, and phrases to use

- How best to determine whether the other person is willing to help

- How to keep the conversation on track

- How to conscientiously convince others to provide information you need

- How to "give something back" so your contacts don't feel like they are doing you a one-way favor (this is *extremely* important)

This chapter offers tips and advice to help better manage phone contacts; person-to-person meetings; the "I hate parties, conventions, and professional associations" syndrome; presentations to coworkers and large groups; and travel fears.

Remember that approximately 75 percent of new jobs and careers are found through networking. And although you should utilize every job-search tactic—search firms, newspaper ads, direct mail, and so on—the majority of your time and effort should be directed toward developing and managing your network.

The career management process includes:

- Personal and career assessment

- Preparation of the marketing campaign

- Implementation of the marketing campaign (network management)

- Job or career decision

Depending on the type of career, experience, salary, and position level, individuals can expect to spend varying amounts of time—from three months to a year or more—finding the most appropriate new job or career. What varies little for all is the percentage of time spent in each phase.

Assessment 15%	Preparation of Marketing Campaign 15%	Marketing Campaign (Network Management) 60%	Career Decision Acceptance 10%

Shy People and Networking

Most seasoned job seekers find their next jobs through referrals from professional colleagues and friends. Networking is often a distasteful activity for shy and introverted people, as it puts them in the embarrassing position of having to ask others for favors and facing the possibility of rejection. Many shy people will do all they can to avoid being put into this uncomfortable situation. This avoidance of personal contacts includes overuse of the following impersonal or formal job search techniques, which are highly inefficient and time-consuming in comparison to networking:

- Responding to classified ads

- Using recruiters

- Returning to school placement offices

Building Relationships — Not Selling Your Soul

Network management is about building relationships, and relationships are built by communicating trust and mutual support.

People will agree to see you for their own reasons, not because you need a job. Their motives for meeting with you can usually be categorized as either personal or professional.

Personal Motives

- *Empathy:* People have other friends or family members also looking for employment, or they remember their own difficulties in finding a job. They want to be helpful.

- *Friendship:* People will do anything for someone referred to them by a good friend. (That's why networking works.)

- *Self-esteem:* People like to contribute to others, particularly by sharing their accomplishments and career progressions they are proud of. You offer them a chance to talk about themselves.

- *Common interest:* People enjoy talking with others who share a common business, social, or educational interest.

Professional Motives

- *Unpublicized job openings:* People know their organization plans to create new jobs, to terminate employees, or to expand through growth.

- *Hidden agendas:* People know family members, friends, or business organizations who are looking for new employees.

- *Specific benefit:* People are stimulated by your background or by what you tell them about yourself.

The Necessity of Face-to-Face Meetings

Effective network management requires face-to-face meetings with contacts. These meetings spin a web of success. The magic of networking includes scheduling face-to-face appointments both with people from whom you are asking for help in the job search process and with people who have no apparent relation to your job search—but who often end up being very helpful. One meeting at 10 A.M. at a particular location allows you to immediately schedule breakfast and luncheon appointments nearby.

Daily face-to-face meetings in the marketplace are an essential requirement for successful network management. Create reasons to meet with people, and get out of your apartment or office on a daily basis. If you are an introvert, this is the hardest part—meeting new people is one of your least favorite things to do! However, this job search may be the only time in your life you are able to catch up with friends, re-establish professional relationships, spend time with volunteer organizations, contact old hobby or sports friends, and build a network of contacts that will enrich your life in years to come—and help you find a new career as quickly as possible.

Communicating Trust

People will meet with you if they trust you and they trust their own decision to spend time with you. *How* you request a meeting is thus as important as *why* you are asking to meet.

People avoid network meetings for a number of reasons:

- They are too busy.

- They see too little benefit in the meeting.

- They don't appreciate your approach.

- They have only a vague understanding about your reason for meeting.

Notice that three out of four reasons are results of poor communication. No one is too busy for a fifteen- to thirty-minute meeting if it is convenient for them and if they think they will benefit from it in some way.

Therefore, you must clearly communicate, particularly on the telephone, to convince people to meet with you. People will often feel comfortable with you, trust you, and agree to meet you:

- To understand your relationship with the networking contact

- To gain clarity about your job focus and reasons for your search

- To respond to a specific request for help

- Because you're respectful of their time

- To offer feedback

Your communications must be clear, direct, and informative in all phases of your search.

Getting the Appointment by Telephone

Successful scheduling of face-to-face appointments through telephone calls depends upon a four-step process:

1. *Tell the truth.* People hear what you say and what you do not say over the telephone. That is why clarity is essential. People hear confidence, friendliness, assertiveness. They also hear tentativeness. Practice and belief in your words and your resume accomplishments will promote clarity.

   Here's a sample:

   > Ms. Jones, Becky Smith, who I'm on the AWED board of directors with, suggested I call. She told me that you know the industry well and might be willing to give me some advice on my career goals now that I'm leaving ABC Industries. She didn't at all suggest that you might know of a job, and that's not the reason I'm calling. I'd really appreciate about a half hour of your time to tell you a little about my background and get your advice about some of the career options I'm thinking about.

2. *Stop talking and listen.* Once you have completed your introduction, listen to what the other person says and does not say. Practice active listening:

- Clarify his or her reply.

- Get more information (keep the person talking).

- Indicate that you heard him or her.

Remember, the person on the other end of the phone is more than likely an extrovert. It's important to try to build trust during this communication. For example, Mary Jones's response to your opening statement may be, "Ok, I have a few minutes—shoot." Proving you heard her right might require a statement that reflects both what she said and, more importantly, how she said it: "I appreciate your willingness to take time right now to be of help."

3. *Get in step.* Prove you heard what your contact said. If you continually demonstrate to your contacts that you are listening to them, they will be more willing to listen to you. *This is the key to successful communication* and requires daily practice. Getting in step initially seems awkward because it sounds like we are accepting bad news. But pay attention—this is the most difficult part for introverts. In fact, most introverts would rather have a root canal than have the following kind of a conversation:

Contact: "I'm sorry, we really don't have any openings at this time."

Your reply: "I can appreciate that when you have no openings, seeing people might be counterproductive, but . . ."

Contact: "Send me your resume, and we will keep it on file." (Said lightly, with little commitment.)

Your reply: "Well, I appreciate your willingness to look at my resume. However, . . ."

Getting in step is essential because it tells your contact you heard and respect his or her reply. After hearing your respect and acknowledgment, your contact will be more willing to listen to the fourth step to getting appointments.

4. *Add a benefit and make a request.* Adding a benefit requires that you offer the contact additional information or reasons of personal interest to see you:

I can appreciate that when you have no openings, seeing people might seem counterproductive. But from the research on your industry that I have done and from what Becky has said about your credibility and contribution to the industry, I know you would be a really good person for me to speak with. I have read a few of your articles (or books, reports, etc.). Thus, I'd appreciate a half hour so you'll know me personally. When would be a good time for you?

The Gatekeeper

The secretary exists to keep the executive focused on her work rather than taking our phone calls. One way to get past this gatekeeper is to learn his or her name, and get them on your side. "Hi Gwen, it's Fredi Balzano again. I was just wondering if you keep her calendar, and could help me out instead of disturbing her. I'm going to need about half an hour, because Becky Smith said she was the perfect person to talk to. Is early morning better? I can be really flexible about this." By the time you have this conversation with Gwen five times, she's going to be on your side!

Planning the Telephone Call

Never "wing" a telephone call (this cannot be stressed enough). Train yourself to not pick up the phone until you have rehearsed the call in advance. Use a script. Summarize the steps necessary to plan a call. Keep this script on your desk in plain sight next to the phone. Internalize your "two-minute pitch." Attend networking workshops as often as you can, and exchange information with other people mastering network management.

Reneé really applies a number of the techniques that I have been talking about. I asked her, because she manages her own business, whether her introversion has worked for her or against her:

Against me. It is very difficult to pick up the telephone and make cold calls. It's always been difficult for me. But, I have divided the field up into:

- Cold calls

- Warm calls

- Hot calls

And I have gotten to be fairly good at making "warm" calls. I make these calls to someone I know, and, more generically, I have written a letter to them first, and then I follow up with a phone call.

By making this warm call, I have made some form
of contact previously. Making a "hot" call, to people I've known before, has really become a no-
brainer for me. I feel as if I've made a lot of
progress using this technique. If it's a "hot" call
(people I've known before, or people I've been
referred to) I definitely do not have a major problem with it. I already know the person through
connections.

I really have carefully scripted out and prepared
my pitch beforehand. I do it with all of the pauses
and all of the smiles. I know it's partly an act, but
guess what? It works, and whatever works I am
guaranteed to love. I prepare my script in big type,
you can probably see it a half a mile away, but if
that's the way I have to do it, that's the way I have
to do it. I know what I want to say, I know how I
want to say it. If anything, I think I have a tendency
to sound too clinical, or too much as if I am acting. So, once I script it, I then think, where am I
going to pause, what do I want to stress, where am
I going to smile? What am I going to add for
warmth? And I do this on the phone as well. I tape
myself so I can hear myself.

Reneé also follows a management plan when she goes out:

I don't particularly like to go to parties. Because,
again, I'm much better one-on-one or in very small
groups, preferably four or less. I hate small talk.
And I'm not very good at it, but I'm getting much
better. Believe it or not, I even have learned to prepare for these things. I jot some things down on a

Post-It, and post it to the mirror as I'm getting ready. Three to five comments about who I am. This helps as I'm preparing for a marketing call as well. I have conversations I can speak to anyone about.

Reneé cautions against custom-designed conversation topics, however, that are religious or political. "Economics is a good topic to talk about," she muses, "as long as I'm not being too esoteric." Reneé prepares for parties the same way she prepares for networking meetings. And she cleverly tries to come up with two innocuous jokes.

Within her work environment, Reneé told me that she's only comfortable in meetings that are short and sweet and to the point.

> I like meetings that accomplish what they are supposed to accomplish. I do not like informational exchanges, I do not like meetings that go on and on. I don't like problem-solving meetings where ten people are asked their opinion and I wind up with ten different answers. I like brainstorming meetings if they are focused. And to be honest, I think I like brainstorming meetings because I'm the one that usually comes up with most of the ideas.

And does this very methodical woman hang out with her peers after work for a light drink?

> Rarely. Unless the people are very similar to me in terms of education, ambition, latest book read, that sort of stuff. I do not enjoy loud, noisy crowds. And

I particularly despise loud, smoky bars. Crowds
drain me. I like to feel as if we are sitting down and
this is going to be refreshing. Not a continuation
of the crazy day we've had. On a Friday I don't
enjoy going to what I call the "seen and be seen"
bar. I can force myself to do it, but I don't like it.

Reneé did express more interest in going to an outdoor
café, where she feels as if she's part of a group. There she can
spread her work out and have the company of strangers
around her. "Hey! I can bounce my ideas off of the waiters!"
she joked.

But Reneé generally doesn't really like going out after
work. "I'm really tired at the end of the day. I put a lot of
extroverted energy into my day. I have a big commute home."
And we're sure when she gets there, putting her tired feet
onto the welcome mat near her front door, she will need to
recharge.

And what about the relationships these after-work meetings serve to build? "Well yes, they really do serve to build
relationships. And I realize that's what's going on. So I do
force myself to do it," Reneé reflects. And she is considerate
and concerned that she not appear too distant.

I don't want to seem rude or standoffish, but I'll
never be an extrovert. There is a line there and I
have not as yet discovered where the balance is
between work and going out and building relationships. What I'm learning in my later life is that the
key really does lie in the quality of one's relationships. That's something I'm very conscious of right
now. And relationships are not just nine to five or
ten to six. They do spill over into after-hours. I'm

cognizant of this, but I'm still working on getting better at it.

I used to read a lot of self-help books and now I read a lot of theological books on developing relationships. Dale Carnegie is fabulous. He emphasizes speaking concisely, with a point to enliven and entertain.

And with her growing confidence, Reneé said, she has learned how to sell her ideas to other people. And that's a real skill. In fact, we know it's a skill that most introverts have a great deal of trouble with.

Successful Network Management

Network management involves developing and managing a structure of relationships: friends, vendors, clients, and the entire circle of your personal contacts and their contacts. They meet and communicate with you and one another at certain planned and unplanned intervals, and at each meeting share momentary or continuing mutual interests. Put into perspective, people in this network will contribute to your finding a new career by offering you a job—or by referring you to other people, who may offer you a job or refer you to their friends who might offer you a job. These same people will call on you to help them support their favorite charity; years from now, they may help your children get into college or discover a business opportunity for them; they may ask you to sponsor them for membership in your favorite organization . . . and so on. You have been networking for years, but you did not call it that. Now you need to structure the process and manage it to find the best career opportunity in the shortest amount of time.

Natural Resistance to Market Research

Many people (especially introverts) are initially reluctant to begin the market research process.

People who have never had direct selling experience, who may blame themselves for being out of work, who have "too much pride," *who are introverted*, resist networking. In the early phase of their job search, they may:

- Count too much on responding to ads and the other aspects of the search that provide only 20 percent of the jobs available.

- Limit contacts to people who are easy to talk with but not necessarily the most helpful.

- Imagine the results of a contact will cause embarrassment, rejection, or make them appear foolish and unconfident.

Fortunately, these resistances can be reduced greatly by developing the structural and communication skills necessary for network management.

Categorizing Contacts: The Essential First Step to Organize Your Network

The first step in network management is to develop a comprehensive list of every person you have met during your lifetime, organized by categories. Take as many as ten to thirty separate pages of paper; on the top of each page list a category under which people you know can be classified. (Don't write their names yet—just the categories.) The categories are similar for most, and each person will be listed under several different categories. The following examples include some obvious categories:

- Current coworkers

- Past coworkers

- Customers

- Clients

- Vendors

- Salespeople

- Family

- Friends

- College friends

- Professional associates

- Social organizations

- Church/synagogue

- College professors

- College alumni

- Neighbors

- Professionals

- People looking for jobs

- People who just found jobs

- Sports enthusiasts

- Cultural enthusiasts

Setting Goals and Performance Planning

Goals are the backbone of network management. Any imposed change, such as job loss, may reduce our sense of autonomy and self-control. To regain our control requires us to set daily goals with some standard of performance by which to measure the results—and to take specific steps to manage the network process.

The SMART model is an excellent objective goal-setting framework you can follow on a daily, weekly, or monthly basis.

Script: What are you going to talk about?

Muse: Think about your conversation before you pick up the phone.

Articulate: Don't let others run away with your idea.

Rehearse: Practice with friends.

Test: Begin your networking with someone with whom you are comfortable.

These criteria should be used throughout your transition period. Monitor (or have someone else monitor) your progress—for example, the number of phone calls you make per day, the number of interviews you schedule per month, or other benchmarks. One specific, measurable, and realistic daily goal might be to complete five networking phone calls, before 4:30 P.M., resulting in at least one appointment.

Developing a network management plan with dates and benchmarks and managing the plan on a daily basis can provide the necessary structure and support during the transition stage. A major responsibility of a job-search campaign is to continually expand your network of contacts. Setting goals and standards of performance, committed publicly, direct your efforts toward results.

Networking was probably started by a bunch of extroverts for their own purposes! But why should they get all of the good jobs? Why should they make all the money?

Networking-Management Makeover

Ineffective→*Effective* Networking Behavior

Situational Challenge	Ineffective Behavior	Effective Behavior	Beneficial Results
Telephone	Avoidance; voice problems (e.g., choking up)	Prepare written "scripts" and questions	Feel in control; acknowledge own pace
Person-to-person meeting	Avoidance; beating around the bush	Focus and clarify what you want; change attitude (you are *not* showing weakness by asking for help); learn to pace yourself	Expand sphere of influence and connections; feel sense of accomplishment
Business meetings, parties, conventions	Hide in corner	Ask questions; make eye contact; exchange phone numbers	Learn information; make new discoveries; gain new friends and associates
Presentations	Stammer; sweat; stutter; get sick	Prepare, rehearse, and role play; expect "worst-case scenarios"	Acknowledge own competence; build confidence

Continued on next page

Networking-Management Makeover

Ineffective→*Effective* Networking Behavior

Situational Challenge	Ineffective Behavior	Effective Behavior	Beneficial Results
Travel	Cannot possibly get on a plane, arrive in a new place, or meet new people	Take something familiar with you (e.g., a family photo from your desk); buy some flowers on your arrival	New surroundings produce less anxiety

If you're reading this book, you've already taken the most important step toward finding a job in which your introverted personality can flourish. But as I've outlined in this chapter, finding that job requires an entire series of steps, many of which may seem unnatural or distasteful to you. Networking is the most important step in this series. By understanding the nuances of networking, taking this essential step won't seem quite so intimidating. Take hints from the above chart to begin identifying how you can change your behavior and make the transition into networking with ease.

The Great Job Search

*"It's not whether you get knocked down, it's whether
you get up."*

VINCE LOMBARDI

Starting a job search can be overwhelming. Where do you
go? Who can you turn to for help? It's a daunting experience, to say the least.

But the search can be broken down into phases—to help
you see the trees, instead of being intimidated by the whole
scary forest.

In reality there are only three parts of a job search, which
can be translated into three questions:

1. Who are you?

2. Where do you want to go?

3. How are you going to get there?

Analyzing and answering each of these questions is crucial to our pursuit and accomplishment of a meaningful life
direction. And you really have to do some significant soul-searching. If we can begin to truly understand ourselves—

"Know thyself" and "To thine own self be true"—we can more readily appreciate who we are, what we have to offer, and what we're going to do.

Who Are You?

Good question! And although it's sometimes tough, it's always a good question to answer. That's why we start with analytical self-assessment. You are not ready to begin your quest for a new opportunity until you have completed some exercises to clarify your goals, values, strengths, weaknesses, style, and personality. If introversion is your style, you need to complete a "snapshot" of who you are in order to use it to your advantage. So, in order to at least begin to travel down the right path, let's do some work on ourselves.

I have been using the following exercises for many years. They were developed during my employment at Citibank's Career Services unit. My clients have found these exercises cathartic; I hope they prove so for you as well.

I want you to sit down at your computer or use lots of paper and just write. These exercises are just for you—no one else will see them unless you choose to share them. And nothing is written in stone, so let your imagination take over. We'll begin with the Job-Person Match, which will help you understand why I encourage you to work as hard as you can on the exercises. These exercises will help you fill in the "person" side of the equation. When the exercises are completed, you can then begin to draft your "pitch." To sell yourself, you need a strong and effective pitch. And the culmination of these exercises will give you one.

Skills

Let's begin with skills. Obviously it is important for you to know that you have them, that there are things you are good

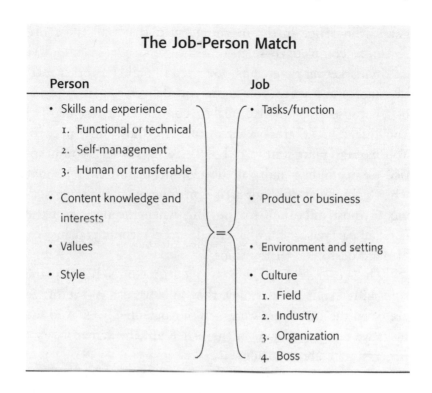

The Job-Person Match

Person	Job
• Skills and experience 1. Functional or technical 2. Self-management 3. Human or transferable	• Tasks/function
• Content knowledge and interests	• Product or business
• Values	• Environment and setting
• Style	• Culture 1. Field 2. Industry 3. Organization 4. Boss

at, and things you would rather not have to do—like networking! *Functional* skills are those given to us by the organization. These are the skills I call the "cocktail party" skills: when you are at a party and a stranger asks, "What do you do?" you usually say, for example, "I'm the vice president of marketing (paper clips) at xyz company."

Marketing paper clips is your *technical* expertise. Telling someone that you market paper clips does not really tell them what you do or how you do it. How you market paper clips, and why you are good at it, does not come up in these "fast-food" cocktail party conversations. The "how you do it" is what we call your *transferable* skills, and rarely do we describe ourselves utilizing our transferable skills. They are considered our "soft" skills, but they are very important. They are the skills that get us up in the morning and ready to get to the job. In fact, if you're not champing at the bit to get to the office in the morning, then that's all the more reason to complete these exercises!

In marketing paper clips, you need to build customer relationships and loyalty. You know you deliver a quality product, because you practice quality control. You test market. You research the areas where paper clips are most needed. You manage your staff. You hold meetings where you practice team building and staff development. You troubleshoot when a shipment does not arrive on time. And customer service is most important to you. But when the person at the cocktail party asks you what you do, rarely would you answer, "I build customer relationships."

These exercises will help you identify your skills set—the soft skills. And, interestingly, the skills we use in the office are often the same ones we use in our personal lives. And the tasks we run away from in the office are the same ones we procrastinate about at home.

For example, I must be the most disorganized person I know. And it's not just that the desk in my office is a mess. My closets are a mess! And the glove compartment of my car is a mess. And I really don't know where anything is. I spend an inordinate amount of time looking for papers I need, business cards people have given me, files, shoes, and clothes I may or may not have gotten back from the cleaners. And I know I could spend any weekend clearing my desk of paper (and sometimes I do, when it becomes ridiculous), but I would rather be thinking big thoughts and solving world crises than filing papers. So I lack organizational skills—but I am a master at listening and solving problems! And I hire great assistants who *are* organized.

Content Knowledge and Interests

How many times have we thought or heard someone else lament, "I'm really good at gardening—but who's going to pay

me to garden?" Well, gardening is one of the fastest-growing
industries in this country, thanks to Martha Stewart. And if
you could not earn a living as a gardener, consider what else
you could do within the gardening industry.

As the following illustration demonstrates, our skills and
interests will always overlap to some degree.

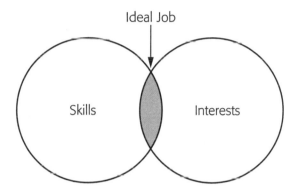

We all have skills, and we all have interests. I happen to
have a borderline psychotic interest in sports (one circle). If
you play it with a ball, I'm there. Basketball, baseball, it
doesn't matter.

Now, I can't perform a slam dunk. But I can use my skills
in coaching and career management to work with ballplayers
who are at the end of their sports careers because of age or
injury. They had a gift but now it's gone, and they need to
find a new purpose. Now, I did a lot of homework on myself
before I realized that I could really work with these athletes—
I found a place where my skills and interests overlapped.

The space where your two circles overlap is where you
will find *your* ideal job. It is the intersection of all of your
unique skills, interests, values, and style. That's why these
exercises are so important. *You can't know where you're going
until you know who you are.*

Values

What is really important to you? Is it working for something you believe in, or earning lots of money? Our values play a very big part in our decision making. And all of life is a trade-off. We have to sacrifice one value in order to live out another.

Let's say a key value of yours is to save the environment. Our planet is being choked by pollution, overpopulation, and waste. Now, given your value system, would you consider networking into a large pharmaceutical or oil corporation? I don't think so. Maybe an organization like Greenpeace is a better choice.

However, let's say that a pharmaceutical company offers you a very large salary with bonuses to come work for them. Now you have a chance to make lots of money and work to try to change the system. Might you now consider that position? See what I mean? We give up some values in order to obtain others.

Style

Introversion can play a significant role in a person's style. Your style, or how you choose to interact with others, for example, will impact your choice of career and particularly your job.

Considering the job side of the Job-Person Match, every job has a task or a function. You are hired to *do* something. Does that task or function match your skills set? If the job is highly detailed and you prefer seeing all possibilities and looking at the big picture, then that particular job is probably not for you. And how does your job relate to your organization's overall business and the products or services it provides?

And, no matter where you work, you will exist in *some* kind of an environment. It could be a cubicle, an outdoor construction site, a classroom, or a corner office. You may have plants and natural light, or work in a windowless basement. Close your eyes and picture *your* ideal environment.

Finally, every organization has a culture. The culture of a hospital is not like the culture of a Wall Street investment banking firm. The people who choose to work in these various cultures are different.

The intersection between the spheres of skills and interests is where you will find your ideal job. When you achieve a job-person match and both sides of the equation balance, you'll know it: you'll wake up in the morning and think, "I can't believe I'm going to get paid to do what I have to do today—this is so much fun!" And most of all, others will cherish you for your introversion.

Work-Related Values Exercise

What is important to you? Your values are continually in flux, so they require constant reassessment. At various stages in your career, you may value money, or leisure time, or independence on the job, or working for something you believe in. I began my career in the not-for-profit world, and now, although I have many clients from that arena, most of my work is in the private sector.

Completing the following list of values will help you clarify what is most important to you now. (For instance, your job may provide you with the freedom and independence you wanted, but not the kind of money your friends on Wall Street are earning.) Consider each item in terms of your overall career objectives and rate its degree of importance using the following scale:

1. Not at all important in my choice of job

2. Not very, but somewhat important

3. Reasonably important

4. Very important

If you wish, add other values to the list or substitute wording you are more comfortable with.

_____ Advancement

_____ Working on the frontiers of knowledge

_____ Authority and responsibility

_____ Helping society

_____ Helping others

_____ Challenges

_____ Working for something you believe in

_____ Public contact

_____ Enjoyable colleagues

_____ Competition

_____ Freedom from worry

_____ Influencing people

_____ Enjoyable work tasks

_____ Working alone

_____ Being an expert

_____ Personal growth and development

_____ Independence

_____ Artistic expression or other forms of creativity

_____ Learning

_____ Location of the workplace

_____ Tranquillity

_____ Salary

_____ Change and variety

_____ Having time for personal life

_____ Fast pace

_____ Power

_____ Adventure/risk taking

_____ Prestige

_____ Moral fulfillment

_____ Recognition from seniors, society, peers

_____ Security and
stability

_____ Chance to make
an impact

_____ Physical work
environment

_____ Clear expectations
and procedures

Of those you marked "4," circle the five *most* important to you today. If forced to compromise on any of these five, which one would you give up? Which one would you be most reluctant to give up?

This is a wonderful exercise to help us realize that life is a series of choices, and we all need to give up some things in order to gain other things. For instance, if one of your top choices is security or stability, you may need to give up money and power. People who really need security in their lives rarely earn lots of money. People who earn lots of money are almost always risk takers.

The following exercise will help you determine whom you want to work for. It was adapted from lectures given by John P. Kotter in his classes in power dynamics at the Harvard Business School.

You and "Bosses"

1. Make a list of all the "bosses" you have ever had in work situations. Include bosses from part-time jobs, summer jobs, and even professors with whom you worked closely.

_____   _____

_____   _____

_____   _____

_____   _____

_____   _____

_____   _____

2. Divide the names above into three lists: those people with whom you had no difficulty, those with whom you had some problems, and those with whom you had severe problems.

No Problems   Some Problems   Severe Problems

_____   _____   _____

_____   _____   _____

_____   _____   _____

_____   _____   _____

_____   _____   _____

_____   _____   _____

3. Look for factors that might help explain why you have had problems with some bosses and not with others (or why you have never had problems). For example, consider:

   • The type of people involved: age, sex, personality

   • The structure of your relationship with the people: how much and what type of power they had over you

   • The broader contexts: the kind of work involved, the type of organizations involved

   • And most important: Were your "problem bosses" extroverts who did not understand your introversion? (It might be helpful to review the management chapter before answering this question.)

Do you see any patterns . . .

   . . . regarding the type of people?

_____

_____

_____

_____

_____

   . . . regarding the structure of the relationship?

_____

_____

_____

_____

_____

   . . . regarding the contexts?

_____

_____

_____

_____

_____

   . . . regarding the introvert-extrovert dynamic?

_____

_____

_____

_____

_____

Satisfiers and Dissatisfiers

For each job you have held in the past, describe as fully as possible those factors that made that job especially exciting or rewarding (*satisfiers*) and those that made that job especially boring or frustrating (*dissatisfiers*). Be as specific as possible (see the example below).

Job	Satisfiers	Dissatisfiers
VP of Manufacturing XYZ Co.	1. Status—large office, staff of twenty-three, Executive Dining Room 2. Fringes—four weeks' vacation, travel allowance, time for outside activities	1. Manager—cold and aloof, little structure or feedback, no organizational credibility 2. Limited professional opportunities—no lateral advancement

Benchmarks

When you think about your career, certain events or episodes probably stand out in your mind—things that led to a lasting change in you. Please identify at least two key events in your career that made a difference in the way you take on assignments now.

1. What happened?

_____

_____

_____

_____

_____

2. What did you learn?

_____

_____

_____

_____

_____

Interests and Subject-Matter Knowledge

1. List below those subjects that you know a fair amount about simply because they interest you. Include subjects and interests from all areas of your life—not only those that apply to work. If you need help getting started or expanding the list, look at sections 2 through 4.

2. Think about the books you read, the magazines you subscribe to, the section of the newspaper you turn to.

3. Think about the volunteer work you do—what are the assignments you enjoy?

4. Think about your hobbies—are there one or two in which you have become so involved that you have built up a lot of expertise and knowledge?

_____   _____

_____   _____

_____   _____

_____   _____

_____   _____

_____   _____

_____   _____

_____   _____

_____   _____

_____   _____

_____   _____

_____   _____

Learning Through Accomplishments

This exercise offers an opportunity to examine the satisfying experiences of your life and discover the skills you want to use in the future. You will be considering the times that you did something particularly well and enjoyed yourself. It doesn't matter what other people thought, whether you were paid, or when in your life the experience took place. All that matters is that you felt happy about doing it, thought you did it well, and experienced a sense of accomplishment.

This exercise usually takes a few days to complete. Many people review different life phases in order to capture the full scope of these experiences. You might want to carry around a piece of paper to jot down ideas as you think of them.

Section I

Briefly list as many satisfying experiences as you can remember. Try to describe concrete examples, situations, and tasks rather than generalized skills or abilities. For example,

- "Successfully met the August 27th commitment deadline" (*not* "Meet deadlines")

- "Coordinated blood drive for the division" (*not* "Coordinating")

- "Completed the New York City Marathon" (*not* "Running")

1. _____

2. _____

3. _____

4. _____

5. _____

6. _____

7. _____

8. _____

9. _____

10. _____

11. _____

12. _____

13. _____

14. _____

15. _____

16. _____

17. _____

18. _____

19. _____

20. _____

21. _____

22. _____

23. _____

24. _____

25. _____

Section II Where Do You Want to Go?

Choose five experiences from Section I that you particularly enjoyed. (Please include at least one non–job-related experience.) For each accomplishment, describe *exactly* what *you* did. Be as specific as possible, listing each step in detail. (Use a separate sheet of paper if necessary.)

Here's how you might begin:

Accomplishment 1

Situation:

Reorganized the work flow in my department.

Actions:

a. Talked to coworkers to determine current work-flow pattern.

b. Wrote description of current work-flow pattern.

c. Designed two alternative methods of organizing work flow—one that cut down on steps and one that broke down the processes into smaller segments.

d. Presented findings and my suggestions to my boss—in writing and in person.

Results:

Got my boss's approval and the go-ahead to try out one of the alternative methods. Rolled out a pilot.

Accomplishment 1

Situation:

Actions:

Results:

Accomplishment 2

Situation:

Actions:

Results:

Accomplishment 3

Situation:

Actions:

Results:

Accomplishment 4

Situation:

Actions:

Results:

Accomplishment 5

Situation:

Actions:

Results:

Section III: How Are You Going to Get There?

Review your five most important accomplishments and use the following list to help you identify the skills you think you used most often. (The list is not comprehensive, so add more skills if necessary.) On the following Skills Assessment Summary, list your most-used skills.

Selection of Skills

Adapt	Budget analysis and review
Administration	Budget planning
Advise	Budget preparation
Analysis	Catalog
Appraise	Client relations
Approve	Coach
Assess	Collect
Assign	Communication
Audit	Community relations

Compute

Conceive

Conceptualize

Conduct

Conflict management

Consult

Contract negotiation

Control

Coordinate

Cost accounting

Cost analysis

Counseling

Create

Crisis intervention

Customer service

Demonstration

Design

Develop rapport

Develop strategy

Development

Diagnosis

Direct

Distribute

Economic research and
   analysis

Edit

Enlarge

Estimate

Expand

Financial analysis

Financial management

Financial planning

Fund-raising

Goal setting

Group facilitation

Human resource
   development

Implement

Improve

Information management

Initiate

Innovation

Instruct

Interview

Invent

Investment consulting

Leadership

Liaison

Listen

Manage

Marketing

Mediation

Motivate

Negotiate

Operations management

Organization

Organizational analysis and
   design

Organization development

Persuasion

Planning

Policy development

Policy formulation

Policy interpretation

Presentation

Preside

Problem analysis

Problem solving

Procedure development	Set priorities
Program design and	Staff development
development	Standard setting
Project development	Strategic planning
Project management	Strengthen
Promotional writing	Supervising
Public relations	Survey
Public speaking	System design
Quality assessment	System development
Recruitment	Task management
Report	Team building
Research	Train
Review	Troubleshoot
Sales management	Visualization
Schedule	Write

Skills Assessment Summary

Accomplishment 1

Skills:

What was your role?

What was your motivation?

What was the environment?

Accomplishment 2

Skills:

What was your role?

What was your motivation?

What was the environment?

Accomplishment 3

Skills:

What was your role?

What was your motivation?

What was the environment?

Accomplishment 4

Skills:

What was your role?

What was your motivation?

What was the environment?

Accomplishment 5

Skills:

What was your role?

What was your motivation?

What was the environment?

Your "Two-Minute Pitch"

Now that you have completed all of the exercises you are ready to think about your *pitch*. Your pitch is the answer to

that question that everyone hates: "Tell me about yourself."
Every interviewer, or the people with whom you network,
will undoubtedly ask this question, or one of the following
variations:

- What can I do for you?

- Why have you come to me?

- How can I help you?

- Why are you looking around?

Use the following tactics to successfully answer these
questions:

- Assume the interviewer wants to know about your
  work—not about you personally.

- Begin with a *headline*—a sentence that tells who you
  are.

- List four or five key skills or qualifications you possess.

- Highlight work experiences(s) that best fit the environment. Illustrate your most impressive accomplishment with a short vignette.

- Discuss your most recent work—it's usually the most
  relevant and most interesting.

- Do not list all the jobs you've ever had.

- Offer more information than your job title and the
  number of years you worked for an organization.

- Base your pitch on what you learned from the skills
  analysis exercises.

- Try to tie the pitch together with your transferable skills.

- Explain why you are looking for a new position.

- Conclude your pitch by asking the interviewer, "Is there anything I've mentioned that you'd like to know more about?"

As stated earlier, you should spend some time on your personal assessment before working on the pitch. Think about an opening line that is a "grabber" for the listener. An interview is really a seduction. You want to "seduce" the interviewer into really hearing what you have to say, because what you have to say is important. Your opening gives them a clue. Here are some examples:

I've changed careers five times. However, the common thread that runs through all of my careers is teaching. I may have exchanged chalk and a blackboard for Magic Markers and a flip chart, but the reality is, I'm a teacher. I help people and organizations learn. Let me give you some examples of my successes.

I'm the kind of person who walks into an organization, takes a look around, and says, "There's got to be a better way to do this" . . . then I begin to figure out how to improve things. Let me give you an example of some of my policy and procedure successes.

I consider myself to be on a mission. I bring a new perspective to every single thing that I do. This is how I've done that in the past.

> I know compensation and benefits better than any-
> one on the planet. It's what I do, it's what I love to
> do. Let me share some stories with you.

It takes some time to develop your pitch, but it is extremely valuable. It really lets the listener know what is at your core: what makes you tick; what makes you get up in the morning—and, most of all, why they need someone like you on board.

Why Two Minutes or Less?

A pitch that exceeds two minutes tends to become unfocused and produce rambling, especially in an introvert. In two minutes, you can communicate the essence of all they need to know. When they need more information, they'll ask!

Think of the pitch as your commercial. Not an infomercial—a commercial. Say you are driving down a highway at 60 MPH and you see a big red sign that tells you that Coca-Cola is a very refreshing drink, with only 140 calories per can and very little fat content and has been in existence for 100 years, the drink of astronauts and kings . . . well, now you have passed the sign, and you barely remember all of that writing—what were they advertising anyway? However, if you're driving down a highway and you see a big red sign with large white letters that say, "Drink Coke!" you may think of that at your next rest stop. That is just like your pitch. "You should hire me!" Period.

Two-Minute Pitch Samples

Here are two examples of pitches that my clients have used. These pitches worked for them. Write a pitch for yourself using these examples as guidelines.

Sample 1

I'm an innovator—an experienced operations manager. I've remade organizations and jobs perceived to be outmoded. I've created new, productive vitality measured by reduced costs, increased efficiencies, and improved morale.

To achieve these results, I've used strong managerial skill, together with problem-solving abilities and factory automation expertise. I'm a creative manager who gets the job done.

In my ten years with Ciba and before then at Squibb, I was responsible for renovating several outdated projects and organizations. In each case, I streamlined operations and reduced costs.

In my most recent assignment, I renovated a facility successfully. As director of packaging and aerosol operations for Acme International, I was faced with departments that were the poorest overall performers of any in the company. In less than two years, I reduced overall operating costs by over $3 million through aggressive programs that increased operating efficiencies by 20 percent, reduced headcount by 18 percent, and improved on-time delivery by 14 percent. In addition, I created positive working relationships among the marketing, finance, and research areas that improved communications and resulted in an improved product for the marketplace. Today, we produce at a 20 percent higher productivity rate, the best in the division.

My talents would be best suited for an operation that requires creativity and an entrepreneurial style. I would be comfortable in a company such as this one, dealing with the consumer in manufacturing or customer service.

Sample 2

I know compensation and benefits better than anyone on the planet. It's what I do, it's what I love to do. I have over ten years' experience helping employees to develop benefit packages appropriate for their individual needs and to make financial decisions for their future. At the same time, I have developed successful employee benefit and pension programs and improved staff productivity.

I owe my success to my ability to analyze and synthesize data and make intuitive decisions. In addition, my excellent communication skills and flexibility make me an effective planner and organizer.

I've held several positions of increasing responsibility in pension and employee benefits administration with the Acme Insurance Group. Previously, I was a job placement specialist with the Cleveland Board of Education.

Most recently, as benefits administrator for Acme, I implemented and marketed a 401(k) profit sharing plan to over 16,000 employees and exceeded company objectives. I also assisted in the automation of the benefits department, which increased productivity by 35 percent.

I am best suited for the administration, policy development, and marketing of creative benefit plans.

This chapter has been devoted to questions pertaining to your self-assessment (who are you?) and your targets (where do you want to go?). At the start of this chapter, I also spoke about the other pressing question: "How are you going to get there?" That is what this book is all about.

First, you need to develop your pitch: the capsule version of your skills and accomplishments that you present to others, the presentation about "you." Then, get out there and talk to people about yourself, utilizing your great pitch! If you decide, for example, that you are really good in technology and marketing, and your dream job would be to work for Microsoft, then you need to speak to people who can help you navigate there—people that can and will help you on your way.

Ask yourself: Who do I know that might know the best friend of Bill Gates? Remember, we are only separated by five or six degrees. By knowing what your skills are, and what you bring to the table, you put yourself in the ready and prepared position to develop your network. Thus, you really do increase your chances to actually pitch yourself to Mr. Gates.

Bear in mind that while delivering a "memorized" script could induce stage-fright tremors for most introverts, this is your script to adapt and play with as you go. As I've said, it tells who you are, where you want to go, and how you're going to get there, and it comes from the extensive homework and practice that you've done. So there's no reason to fear that you'll forget your lines—that would be like forgetting who you are! By now you've done so much research and introspective thinking that forgetting would be impossible.

11

INTROVERSION AND CULTURAL DIVERSITY

"Fans don't boo nobodies."

REGGIE JACKSON

As an introvert, you have now given a great deal of thought to how you communicate, how this differs from the ways in which other people communicate, and how you can bridge the gap between these different styles of communicating. As I've said before, introverts cannot force themselves to become extroverts, and trying to do so would likely result in disaster—not to mention a lack of diversity. If you're an introvert facing this dilemma, overcoming these hurdles can seem overwhelming. But all it takes is identifying what communication habits are causing you problems and deciding whether or not they need adjusting. In this chapter we'll learn effective ways to bridge the gaps created by communication hurdles that are exacerbated by cultural differences.

Emily, for example, coached a *very* senior person in financial services who was exceedingly valued for his technical expertise and knowledge.

He's a very likable man who grew up in a small town and attended a small college and graduate school. He's young and married. He came to me because, when he had to make a sale with two more senior people on his team, he would respond to a question by immediately leaning forward, looking down, and thinking about what had been asked. There were long silences. The other members of the team would fill in the silences, and when my client looked up, the subject had been changed. My client did not want to come up with some kind of knee-jerk reaction; this was contrary to his style and his values. But it was getting him in trouble, and they did not want to take him on sales calls. I needed to help him find a way, while he was engaging in this very rich and creative thinking process, to let the others know that he was still "home" or at least still in the room with them. He also needed to *include* them in the process—whether with a certain gesture or just making eye contact with them.

This man was from a Protestant background where large motor movements were not a part of his repertoire. The others on his team were from Mediterranean cultures, where large gestures are par for the course. Gestures, voice tone, and volume were all a part of this process. My client was out of sync with the others. He needed to learn how he could keep them engaged while he was going through his thought process and do it in a way that he was comfortable with. Not in a "hail fellow, well met" way. But he was coming across as being fairly contemptuous of everyone else. And that *perceived* attitude was getting him into trouble.

This all became part of what he needed to do to change.

We had long sessions and it was a relief for him to feel that someone was thinking of ways to help him bridge the gap. We developed a tool kit of techniques he could use to be more expansive. We videotaped him. The end result was that in his new business presentations, he was able to expand his own repertoire and become more successful.

I once coached a guy from Italy. He had a Harvard M.B.A. He would go out to make these presentations to Procter and Gamble to all of these Wasps. And he was always using his hands. He wanted to stop using his hands. That, of course, would not work because it would take away who he was. But he was able to learn how to make smaller gestures. It made a huge difference in his presentations. That's a dramatic example of cultural differences.

I now have a female Asian-American client, who came here as an immigrant. I have a good relationship with her. She is very concerned that if she does not do as I say she will be treating me disrespectfully. But to her, networking means asking for something and showing signs of weakness. So here I am with all of these good ideas, but I have had to temper the way I present them to her. I put an idea on the table, we look at it, and then put it aside and maybe we'll return to it later. So, the idea gets thrown out there, so she can process it internally and maybe use it or not in a time frame that makes sense to her.

What did not work for this client was to try to include her spouse—in terms of what *she* wanted to do versus what *he* wanted to do. He did not want to be included in any kind of spouse-coaching at all. This just is not done in their culture.

There are things within her culture that place her into a very introverted role. But within her community, she is considered very extroverted. *She* is the one people call on for advice.

"Wow," I commented. "This is so interesting. So if we take her ability within the community to be social and translate that into some kind of networking, she could be an interpreter."

"Yes," Emily responded, "you're absolutely right. One of the things I learned from working with her is that I needed to take a lot of time. As an extrovert, my rhythm is so fast, and in this instance, with this client, I really needed to slow down. It enables me to listen better, so I am learning from her. But I don't know how far we will get with the concept of networking. She loves—has a passion for—fashion, and she's gone to her favorite department store and filled out an application. But that's all I have been able to get her to do."

Stacey describes a different experience in explaining her comfort level when confronted with ethnicity:

I tend not to speak on diversity issues because including me there are only three black people in my whole organization, so *I'm* speaking from the "black point of view." At the last meeting, however, I finally spoke out. This was a rarity, but I had to. The question was pressing. But, due to the race factor, I did feel uneasy about possible negative consequences. That concern, coupled with my introversion, could have easily kept me from speaking. I feel as if I'm stuck between a rock and a hard place—between race and introversion. I feel as if I'm boxed in.

I sat in on another meeting. Again, I said nothing because all of the information was about the planning process and the strategy of the organization and how there was a vision to pay attention to the individual. Truth be told, I kept thinking: "How are they going to make all of these big plans when three-fourths of the people in this room don't really care about these individuals? They don't even *like* the people." Or, in another example, my boss may have plans for me to be the next program officer, but if the people above her don't like her (because of skin color or race, or anything), then she has no ability to work on a promotion for me. Therefore, I will not be the next program officer. So, once again, I don't speak.

Christopher describes his own experience with diversity:

What was lethal for me as an introvert was my experience in the jazz world. I started out as a musician in an age when the bands that had been integrated began to segregate again. As a white guy and an introvert, I had to really push to be accepted in the New York jazz scene, which was made up mostly of African-American and Latino people. I did not want to play white jazz. I thought of that as a very inferior and derivative form. I wanted to aim for the real thing. I thought that the intellectual significance of jazz would be more important than my middling success as a jazz player and playing the color line. There was some room for a white guy who was a bassist. There could be an all-black band with a white bassist. The whole idea of jazz for me was this idea of continually making it up. You develop this facility to be articulate, and the goal is to avoid repetition. So it is a sort of endless creativity. In jazz you kind of have a "bad" attitude that is caused by the sense that you have developed this incredible articulate auditory facility but there is no commercial potential. There is no way for you to show what you can do. You are not required to do it if you play a wedding. You're not really allowed to do it on the "job." They don't want you to play the hits that somebody else had. The customers are not that interested in stuff that's been done.

But as a scientist now, I carry that attitude with me that there is a lot of very ordinary work that is out there. What makes science good is that the secondary work is always useful, but what I wanted to do was the "jazz" of science: to prove that it is possible to do a virtuoso piece, not merely a plausible rendition of what had already been done. I wanted to do something that was original—that would really make people take notice.

What's lucky for me is that I've had that ambition, I've had the view of my imagination—being very different from the ordinary—and I have been able to move my specialty field toward me. I have lots of fans. I don't have a false view of my importance. Science is not like jazz, where there are four or five players at a time and one leads the charge and the others chime in. But I have been able to

realize that the thing I started out to do, I have
been able to do very well. In science, I get people
to learn the tune that I wrote—that is more difficult than the tune that they wrote. This is an exten-
sion of my arrogance. As a jazz musician, I knew
also that I could leave the village Vanguard and go
up to Manhattan College. That was also a part of
the arrogance. I have no failures.

Cecilia, who is from England, has yet another perspective on diversity:

Because of my accent, I think that I am perceived
as arrogant. And I'm really not! In America, which
is far different from England, there is an incredible disconnect. When I first came to America, I
was working in a company with another college
friend from home. We would get together with others in the company and they did not understand our
sense of humor, our jokes, or our sarcasm. They
did not understand that we were being funny and
not taking things seriously, just like them. When
you're being jovial, and others are not getting it, I
think that's difficult. I don't know how to be easy,
because of my introversion. I don't know how to
walk into a room and connect with the ease that
other people do. The natural assumption on my
part is that I'm going to bother people—but if they
approach me, then that's OK. I'm happy and excited,
but I still feel that I don't want to bother them.
Then they feel that I'm *really* arrogant, and they
perceive it as being standoffish. I think a part of

this is that I must reject them before they reject me. So I will just go do my own thing. Then I proceed to look desperately busy, rather than looking like this poor soul who really wants to be accepted by the crowd.

I also discovered that I'm very bad at job searching. In the early days, after coming to America, I did a fair amount of job seeking and I always got into trouble because I didn't have a green card. I finally found a company that would sponsor me. It's a fairly easy process, but companies do not like to go through the expense of lawyers, and so on unless they feel you are absolutely exceptional. So that has put me where I am. I've been negligent trying to pursue other work, because I don't have a green card. I did get called by a headhunter, and I just blew it off, because I come with the additional problem of not having a green card. If I was a bit more extroverted and a wheeler and dealer, I'm sure I could find a way. Those extroverted people always do. My current company is willing to sponsor me, but I have to pay for it, and it costs $6,000. Plus, everyone else in America can do marketing, and I could only get a sponsor if the company could prove that I had a skill no one else had.

Cecilia doesn't know if she will do a lot of networking when looking for her next job because she feels she is terrible at it. But her visa expires in two years, and because her current company is having financial problems, she will need to find another position soon or go back to England. To stay in this country, Cecilia will have to network.

Carolyn has played an important role in cultural diversity:

> I was one of the first groups to be bused in Queens, New York (back in the 1950s). I came from my insulated black neighborhood to an all-white, Jewish community. There were only one, or maybe two, black kids in each class. From the age of eight, I learned to perform. Because then the teacher would give me the pat on the shoulder: "Oh, isn't that good." As long as I performed for my white teachers, I was fine. Well, that is not true. I was always uncomfortable with it. I didn't even have to study. All I had to do was perform.

Carolyn found that in suppressing her own cultural identity in order to fit in or communicate with the culture in which she went to school, she also suppressed her ability to learn. She spent so much time learning to behave like everyone else that she wasn't able to take advantage of her education. Granted, in that time period, she had no alternatives. But as we can learn from the other examples in this chapter, it isn't necessary to abandon culturally diverse ways of communicating anymore. Rather, we need to identify these cultural differences and adapt them when talking to someone of another culture so that we are better understood. It's like learning another language. You don't have to forget your own language; you just have to include other people's ways of communicating.

(12)

GENDER: CAN REAL MEN BE INTROVERTS?

"We made too many wrong mistakes."

YOGI BERRA

Is our late twentieth-century society becoming increasingly supportive of the sensitive male, or in fact do we live in a culture where the "macho" image is the norm? If, in fact, males have to portray that "Macho, Macho Man," how does the introverted style fit that image?

In sports, we see lots of examples of this. Consider what they say about hockey: "There was a huge fight and then, all of a sudden, a hockey game broke out!"

Most research studies show vast differences between males and females (Balzano 1995). These differences are noticed from infancy, where males are observed as being more aggressive. We know that girls in school often tend to be overlooked and emerge from adolescence with a poor self-image, relatively low expectations from life, and much less confidence in themselves than boys (Gilligan 1982). In a survey commissioned by the American Association of University Women, it was found that boys, too, lost some sense of self-worth in school—but they ended up far ahead of the girls. The study concluded that girls with higher self-esteems drew their strength from family and community rather than from the school system. But the school system is a structured environment, supposedly preparing students for success in organizations. If girls can't thrive in schools, how can women thrive in organizations? This is the start of the proverbial "glass ceiling."

Fact is, women account for as many as half of the professional employees in the latest industrial and service companies, yet they hold fewer than 5 percent of the senior management positions. And most of the senior jobs women do hold are in such areas as human resources, finance, or public relations. Executives agree that women need to become more assertive about breaking through barriers and seeking important line positions, such as general manager of sales and marketing or heading other business units like manufacturing. These positions have traditionally been held by men, who reject relinquishing them. However, women aren't the only victims of glass walls and ceilings. It is becoming an issue for men as well. *All* executives have to learn enough cross-functional skills so they can mature into general managers. Everyone now has to manage their own careers; people no longer receive promotions based solely on tenure. The only way to manage your cross-functional training and discover what you have to do next to receive that promotion is to get out there and talk to people: network, network, network.

Do men, then, have an advantage in the world of shmoozing and networking because they have been taught from day one that the world is theirs? Well, it depends. I have interviewed and worked with many males who admitted to being introverted and shy. And we know these traits can be a hindrance, as the men in the following case studies demonstrate. They discuss their various experiences, and share effective self-management improvements. The men in the following interviews are very different, yet all are considered to be very successful. All feel as if their introversion has held them back in their respective careers.

Both males and females can gain a more assertive business profile by becoming more visible and vocal. Help people to get to know you, as discussed in Chapter 4. This chapter highlights ways to utilize networking.

But, first, consider how a statement made by Stacey about her husband illustrates some of the male stereotypes concerning their personalities and aggressive behavior: "My husband is only an extrovert when he's doing karate. But when he's not, he's really an introvert. He just thinks he's 'Mr. Man,' but he's really an introvert." (Actually, karate may not be that extroverted; there's a lot of grunting, but also a lot of introverted self-discipline. And, ironically, karate originated in a culture that is certainly more introverted than that of the United States.)

I think Stacey's assessment of her husband says a lot about what many people generally think of introverted versus extroverted men. Is it fair? Probably not. Although the men in the following passages express strength and confidence, they also relate their fears and concerns that introversion has in some way hindered their growth and pursuit of their careers.

Steve is a prominent lawyer, an introvert, and a cool observer. Steve came to me when he was "of counsel" in a firm. However, the firm wanted him to become a member and gave him an ultimatum: "Integrate into the firm or get out." So, while he was negotiating with them, he looked around for another place. At one point he had actually found a new opportunity—a nice little firm that would have taken him on "of counsel." One of their partners, who is an extrovert and a trial attorney, suggested that Steve just talk to his current firm and tell them what he was feeling. That had absolutely never occurred to Steve. He admitted being very afraid of change. Thinking about what he should do, and asking himself some key questions regarding his future direction, he approached his firm: "Listen, I think you want me to be available, exclusively, for the firm, and I don't want to be restricted. I have my own clients, so this is not going to work. My portable business is important to me," Steve said, determined to express his strong feelings. And lo and behold, they agreed to keep him on "of counsel."

But some things haven't changed all that much. Steve went on to explain his awareness of his personality type.

"I have always been aware of my shyness or introversion. It ran in my family. Growing up, I was totally introverted and always alone. I grew up in New York—Far Rockaway, Queens—and had no brothers or sisters. I used to like to go to the playground and play ball, but I would say that my parents did not promote the idea of my being with other people. I became a history teacher and was in graduate school, teaching in Brooklyn so I would not have to go to Vietnam, and because I had nothing else to do. I was drawn to law school because I knew I was not going to be a teacher forever, and at that point in my life there was not a whole lot that I was drawn to.

One day my father asked, "How do you like teaching?" And I said, "I hate it." He said, "So what else are you going to do?" I answered, "I'm going to law school." There was not a whole lot of thought that went into the choice. I just did it. I went to law school at night and I taught during the day. And I did well in law school, but when law school was over I realized I was terrible at interviews. I ended up getting a job at Merrill Lynch, through a friend, but the law department was a Fordham Irish bastion and I'm Jewish! So I left, and another friend helped me get a job with the Securities and Exchange Commission (SEC).

I got to Montgomery (my current law firm) because I knew Mr. Montgomery socially. It wasn't working out at the previous job, so he brought me on.

But introversion has absolutely held me back in terms of my career—because I'm not aggressive enough in going after business or doing the marketing. There is a certain amount of effort that goes into that, and it's very hard for me to follow up. And it's very hard for me to make a second call.

I always wonder: How often should you call? Once a week? Once a month? When I'm pushed, I'll do it. If I'm going on a call *with* someone, I'll do it. But to make calls myself . . . it's very hard. Though I think I'm very good at establishing relationships with people who become my clients, I'm not good at maintaining them. But I'm great at establishing them!

I know a million people, but I don't call them. My wife and I joined this very swanky tennis club and I met and play tennis with the president of a very large investment firm. Even though we had him over for dinner last summer, I haven't spoken to him all winter. Now it's summer again and I saw him last weekend at the club. He's an extrovert, or at least more extroverted than I am, and my very extroverted wife said, "Why don't you go talk to him?" And I felt like, "What am I going to say to him?" I guess I would if I saw an opening, but I can't "cold call" him.

I reminded Steve, "That wouldn't be cold calling. You play tennis with the man. You know him." Steve's defensive reply emphasizes how painful networking can be for introverts:

You're right. You're right. I don't know if this is just a road block I'm using, but I just really don't want to do anything right now.

Even now, because I think that this whole new deal I made at Montgomery may be unraveling, I may have to go out and talk again, and I really don't want to do it. I know how to do it, but I don't want to, not just because of being an introvert, but because I know everyone in this office. Anxiety, as well as inertia, develops. It's like you're looking for something and you have to wade through so much garbage to find the gem you're searching for. Plus, networking is so time-consuming, and I have so many other things I could be doing, like washing my hair!

But if it does not work out at Montgomery, then I really do want to see how many of my clients I can keep, and move out to Long Island. I like law. I don't think I'm passionate about it, but I have a tremendous amount of expertise in my practice area. I hate what I see happening to the law though. There is a dumbing-down of the law, especially in my area. I don't know what would be a passion for me. But I'm lucky in the sense that I get to practice the part of the law that I *do* like and that I do best.

In my heart of hearts I know what I should be doing. It's like marriage. You want to find love, but so much involves someone trying to see how much *they* can unload on *you*. Luckily my clients are self-

> referrals, because I do a damn good job. I will need
> to do some networking very soon though, and I am
> not looking forward to it. I am just not comfort-
> able in the networking process—not at all.

Steve has been honest with himself, and with me. His career has actually been quite good (for him and to him). He's found a niche and has been both financially and personally successful, but feels he could be even more successful if he could be more aggressive in his approach to networking. Remember, attributes our "all-American" culture reveres are dominance, assertiveness, leadership, independence, and risk-taking. Hence, out of ignorance, a stigma often shadows shyness and introversion. Individuals that are sociable, active, and expressive capture a lot of attention. And people who are able to garner attention and feel at ease with it, such as actors, athletes, and other high-profile personalities, are most likely to be successful.

Christopher, the former jazz musician, has never been a client of mine; I met him through his wife, my colleague and an extrovert. He explained his introversion has affected his personal life and career in technology to help the deaf people suffering from brain-injury trauma, and adults who have lost the ability to speak to communicate.

Driven by technology, he skillfully uses the computer keyboard, soon to be replaced by a microphone, which is a specialized tool developed for the field. (And in this field, this is where the money comes from.)

> I have always been aware of my introversion; I've
> always been socially aware, and I've never had much
> difficulty understanding the motives of others at
> the point of social contact. But it's consistently

surprised me how unusual my experiences with other people are. The key to my introversion is that my natural mode of interaction with people, my natural mode of experiencing the world, is to think about it.

I realized that I was a little bit different when it came to thinking fast about things and drawing conclusions or forming impressions very readily. And I have always been a very avid reader, while lots of people are not. In fact, when I have a moment that is uncommitted, I will think of reading something rather than picking up the telephone to call someone. Reading gives me a form of pleasure and comfort, that form of solitary experience that is just different.

I always saw this part of myself as a strength and not a weakness. It was not "a difference" that made me feel bad. I'm not even sure that my character has changed very much from childhood. I have a feeling that the way I am now and the way I was as a child is not that different, and both my mother and father agree. And though I was not an only child, I was the oldest of four, which made me an only child for awhile. Then, later, I became the third parent to my younger siblings.

Once the other kids were born, I no longer had refuge. I felt that my privacy was continually invaded, not just by my brothers and sisters, but also by my parents. I had to be prepared for interruptions at all times. As a kid I would always hear: "Why are you sitting in the house?" But when my siblings were out playing, that would be the only time I would have some solitude!

But I did play, and I had a lot of friends. And we did the typical kinds of stupid stuff that boys do. There was a group that I played touch football with. And there was a group that I played softball with. There was also a group that I played "Michigan Rummy" with on rainy days. And I appreciated growing up in Stuyvesant Town and in Mount Vernon, New York, since my mother grew up over a grocery store in the more urban environment of Brooklyn and always wanted her own yard and her own grass to put her toes in.

When I think about whether my introversion has held me back, I conclude that it is a question of mythology, my personal mythology. I had a couple of good opportunities. And I enjoy my career very much; I receive a lot of recognition. And I'm not saying that being an introvert held me back in the sense that I would have hit a higher point; I think I have done as well as anyone in my generation, so this is not a "sour grapes" story.

I do all of my own work. I chose a kind of institution where I would be responsible for not only the work, but for providing my own infrastructure, which means that although I have the pride of accomplishing many simple, rudimentary tasks, the thing I get my reward for is the thing that I do once I complete the infrastructure. It's a kind of mom-and-pop store that I have built here as a researcher, in which if we need a cable, there is no engineer on board to ask, "Would you get the cable?" I have to make the cable up myself.

I am running a much smaller operation than what a well-networked extrovert would. A well-networked extrovert would have a far more "corporatized" operation here. There are other labs in my institution that do run that way. And I have occasionally had to burn the midnight oil (I have all the righteousness that all self-sacrificing people have). But I understand that this has been a cost to me, and I would rather pay the cost through my own solitary labor than to pay the cost of having all of these other people whose lives I would have to manage. Sometimes, I wonder what the other hidden costs are that I don't even think about—an inability to reach out, an intellectual life that comes from *Mad* magazine, and the irreverence that comes from the "ordinary." There is an arrogance that says, "I don't really need you anyway, and I'm smarter than you. And I can get it done by myself—and better—so what do I need you for?" And then I wind up by myself, doing more work than any sane person should have to do.

Nat is currently working for a large, New York City–based real estate firm. His position is to analyze the company, crunch the numbers, and find areas where the company has placed itself at risk. If the numbers or the particular real estate deal do not look good, he is obligated to express concern and point out the ways the company could face bankruptcy. Nat is under a lot of stress because his organization could, once again, be on the verge of bankruptcy.

Nat was not really aware of his introversion per se while growing up. However, he was always aware that he was different.

I've always felt that I attack a problem from a different angle. And it may be intuitive instead of introverted. My product, even in high school, was different from the others. When the teacher would give an assignment, the other kids would write what the teacher espoused, and I would do something completely different. Some teachers liked that. Some teachers wanted exactly what they asked for, letter by letter. It didn't happen that often, but sometimes I got into trouble. But usually I was not penalized for it.

I was always aware that I did things differently, but I was not aware of introversion at that level. I think my parents were introverts as well. They assisted me in doing things. But my early concept of introverts was probably having a lack of friends and not running around in large groups.

I can't say that I felt, prior to high school, less of a swinger than anyone else. I didn't curl up and read a book. I was out playing. I got into trouble if I were to stay home and read a book. I also remember, in high school, or maybe in junior high, I became uncomfortable at dances and parties. Up until that point I always felt that I was in control of things. In retrospect, a lot of the kids I ran around with were younger than I was by about one or two years. I was the leader. So I matured faster than other kids. But once the other kids caught up with me, then I began to experience some uncomfortableness.

I wasn't great at sports, but I did ok at other activities. And I was fairly aggressive when it came to getting brownie points from the teachers.

In the work environment, I'm quite comfortable with my coworkers, especially those of an equal or peer level. I'm comfortable with superiors as long as I don't see them as equals. There's one superior that I'm thinking of. As long as we sat down daily and I got feedback and responses, in terms of what's going on, I felt comfortable. But that communication link dried up, and it's now become very uncomfortable. Communication is a vital link.

Nat explained that his relationship with his current boss is deteriorating due to unspoken changes in the organization.

Formerly there was a trust level in which I could say, "hey I don't know how to do this, how should we handle this?" and I could get an unbiased answer. But now, that old communication has changed to an aggressive and superior "I am going to pull rank on you" style. He has become a member of the "sitting up while looking down on you" club. And *he* has the same relationship with *his* boss. That same superior versus inferior relationship spills down into our relationship. He's modeling himself after that, and so things have changed between us. Now, it has become an aggressive situation where the assumption is that everything I do is incorrect until proven otherwise—whereas before, our modus operandi showed our willingness to apply a "let's work it out" orientation. So, things are certainly tense in the organization, and because of my introversion I'm not demanding the feedback that I need.

Before, even in this tense environment, I could ask for feedback. Now, things have deteriorated. If I were someone other than who I am, I could demand better feedback. Now I find it impossible. And I've gone from most favored to least favored employee, because I'm not a "hail fellow, well met good ol' boy." If I could schmooze, I think things would be different. Or, if I were more aggressive.

Aggressiveness in this organization is admired. I am not an aggressive person. With me, it's not the end product. It's how you can look in the boss's eyes. From a management perspective, if you feed them hogwash and it makes them and the organization look good, they're happy. If you feed them the truth and it makes them or the organization look bad, then you are in trouble.

If one is a good "pat-him-on-the-back boy," one does well in the organization. But don't tell anyone anything they *don't* want to hear. The employee who feeds them a cock-and-bull story is the one who gets ahead.

As far as going out after work, I would go out for drinks with peers. I enjoy that. Anything that is multilevel, however, I have no interest in—like the Christmas party. I go to the Christmas party, and I get out as quickly as I can. I go because it's political to go. Because of a lack of communication on my part as well as on senior management's part, and the lack of networking—I don't network in the company—I'm sure my introversion has held me back in my career. But this is something I'm aware of and working on.

When I go to meetings, lots of times my goal is not to stick out, not to put my neck on the line. When I do contribute, I contribute from my heart and try to be constructive to the organization. If I find my contributions are not acknowledged or appreciated, then I will just sit back and listen. I do care to be supportive of what's going on, but I want to be supported as well. I don't believe in shooting people down. I don't believe in aggressive behavior. I will raise questions if things are not great, but if someone comes up with an idea that presents a possibility, I say go with it, rather than come up with reasons not to go with it.

Learning about my introversion at the start of this current job search has been extremely valuable. The results from the Myers-Briggs Type Indicator got me thinking. It improved my thinking process. It justified a lot of questions that I had. Did it give me answers? No. Did it give me a push into thinking in new and expanded ways? Yes. And ultimately, I came up with some very real and strong answers. Which, by the way, were not solely based on just my experiences.

Going back to networking for a moment, my first reaction to it took me back to my past experiences as a life-insurance salesperson. That's what networking was, and I was a failure. I had a strong "Oh no, here we go again" attitude. Not that I couldn't do it. I didn't *want* to do it. I would compare this to running through a field of people with the bubonic plague to rescue a child. There is a very good reason to do it. All is not negative. There is *a lot* that is positive, but you have to go through a lot of negatives to get there.

And I'm sure that introversion and the lack of networking can impact one's credibility. Maybe sometimes I'm lacking when it comes to opening up, because I only open up when I feel sincere or fairly certain about something. On a surface level, I would think that would add to my credibility. Being the numbers guy, I'm not going to tell you what you want to hear. I'm going to tell you the truth. If I know something is numerically wrong,

I'm not going to tell you about it. I'm going to go fix it and tell you about the corrected one. To me, this should add to credibility. But it depends on who's demanding the information. My boss has two different motives. One, he wants to be able to sit on the witness stand ten years from now and say "this number was right to the best of my knowledge." But two, he also has to sit in *his* boss's office and say "this number is correct," knowing it's wrong. Many times I can't tell which boss I'm dealing with. Then here I am feeling like I'm caught between a rock and a hard place.

When *I'm* in the "manager" role, I work very well with those who are reporting to me. I'm clear. I'm credible. Feedback from those who work for me is that *I'm clear*. From people that are not directly underneath me (my boss's peers), I get feedback that they don't understand my work. These are superiors. And from a former peer, who is now at the next level, *I feel* that I really give him the information the way I know he can understand it. We worked together in the past, and I know he's very technical. Yet he now claims not to understand. When someone is willing to sit back and analyze my work, I feel it couldn't be clearer. But if one glosses over it, then it's not clear. It has to be analyzed.

Nat has some fears about networking, but hopes that it will become easier as he narrows and defines his "targets" and he gets closer to an industry about which he feels more passionate: financial planning.

I'm still looking for my next position, but I am taking some advanced courses in financial planning that will help me achieve my next step. I've also recently done some job-related networking and I felt OK about it. I did not initiate the meeting; the meeting just fell into place. He was very supportive. He did not give me any additional names, but I know I have to get a lot more aggressive about networking as my current job winds down.

I expect that networking will become easier because I will not be involved in real estate. In fact, I had a lead yesterday for a real estate position, and I looked really hard to find the link that disqualified me for that position so I could turn it down. I hope that the closer I get to financial planning, the easier the networking will be. I know it, I know how to do it, I even think I *can* do it. I just don't want to do it. I have to *want* to do it. I have to pierce my comfort zone to the point where I know that I have to do it and it becomes my number one priority.

Yes, I have fears of the future, and I know I have to take risks. Just where I have to take those risks, I have not decided as yet.

I also realize how much my introversion manages to impact my personal life. I don't have close friends. In the past if I had friends it's been one. Most of the people I deal with are business relationships. I deal very well in a religious organization. A few years back I was chair of the finance committee of my church. I've headed up several other projects for the organization. But everything I've done in the church has been business related. With one possible exception: I took a course on personal religious biography and I managed to get close to those people and feel comfortable with them.

Nat is continuing to carry a difficult course load at New York University in order to become a certified financial planner. We agree that this particular industry will suit Nat's style and personality. He will be able to consult with clients individually, calmly helping them to achieve their financial goals. And his introversion will be a plus.

In many of my "Networking for Introverts" seminars, someone will comment on the fact that there are far more women in the room than men. Thus I am often asked if there are more female introverts than there are male. We do not have raw research data on this yet, however, we do know that many times in our "macho" society, the introvert could be looked upon as being wimpy. This truly is *not* the case. We just need more men to own up to their own introversion.

13

Tying It All Together

"It's like déjà vu all over again."

YOGI BERRA

When I asked Portia whether introversion had ever held her back in her career, she explained that it was a difficult question—partly because when she had career problems in the past, she was not aware of her personality type.

> Maybe if I had known I was an introvert that would have helped me get through the big crises better. But because I did not know, I think I acted out in ways that were not necessary. Looking back, there were probably other ways I could have handled some situations. I had options, but at the time I felt I didn't have any choices. So, yes, I would say that maybe it has held me back.

But Portia went on to say that she thinks her introversion has also helped her career at times.

There *is* a kind of charisma that introverts can cultivate. We are not as accessible as our extroverted coworkers. We don't make every process we are going through obvious. Extroverts therefore find us intriguing, and that can be a very powerful characteristic, even in a leadership role. Sometimes the most effective thing to do is to sit. There is a "spiritual" quality sometimes attributed to introverts—which we may or may not have—because of our ability to stay calm during crisis situations. That ability can be both mysterious and fascinating to more extroverted people. Knowing that you are an introvert and managing yourself and others appropriately will make that charisma all the more powerful.

Making people aware of their personality type much earlier in their career and teaching them the skills they need to manage themselves more effectively would make such a real difference in people's lives. I personally feel as if I spent much of my earlier career stumbling around trying to find out who I was. If I had learned some of this when I was an undergraduate student, or even in graduate school, it would have put me that much further ahead. Had I known about my type sooner I could have been much more proactive about doing things that were against my nature but which were still important things for me to do as a manager. When I was working with board members and employees who didn't understand my "sitting and thinking," and who had a "bias to action," I would have communicated on a regular basis, giving them an opportunity to understand my plans and processes. Even though I might have been anxious and impatient thinking about having to do it, it would have made a tremendous difference in the way things turned out.

Knowing about your personality type also helps in one's choice of work. If I take on a job where I'm going to have to interact with people, it has to be the kind of energy that I am willing to expend. It's not just, Do I have the skills to do this job? but also Do I have the internal *will* to do it? Do I think I can apply my energies in the way I need to for a particular role? It is not just intellectual competence. There are many things I am capable of doing which may not be appropriate to the type of person I am. It is very important to find a comfort level where you can lead or work effectively.

Personality types play an important role in our personal lives as well. For example, learning about my own personality type has helped me think about how to manage my son, who, as I mentioned earlier, is an extrovert. As in the workplace, it is a challenge to realize that this is not a battle of wills or a matter of obedience. It's something that takes conflict into a different arena, one that has more to do with style and skill.

Personal Relationships

Writing this book gave my coauthor Marsha a lot to think about. During this period she began to understand why her long-term marriage and union of twenty-three years had almost always seemed to be in a state of struggle-to-survive, and why it inevitably fell from its course.

I often felt that things just didn't really click for us, and that it had a lot to do with pieces of our personality. We are both two really cool, nice people who deeply care for and love each other, but somehow I felt we didn't nurture each other enough, emotionally and physically. We would fall into these constant ruts; metaphorically, it was almost as though a part of us would die! We wanted to infuse ourselves with *something*, I think, but generally lacked the wherewithal or precise know-how. And our timing was *always* off.

It seems that it took too much energy, and we just didn't have it in great enough amounts to give. Now I've come to understand more about the fact that we both share introverted personality traits, though one much more than the other. And though I was less than enthused by my partner's frequent episodes of quietness—sometimes he would go deeper and deeper inside himself, becoming very reluctant to communicate or share his innermost thoughts—I didn't realize, or perhaps consciously think about, the underlying cause of our "missing it." This didn't really sink in until I took the Myers-Briggs to complement my work on this project. I pondered over the fact that I too have an introverted style, which we all now know affects where, when, and how we process and receive our energy source—so it's understandable that relationships will be affected. Oh, I did know that sometimes I had a quiet side, but things are much clearer now that I have had this opportunity to visit, analyze, and fill myself with so many cases and facts about introversion and extroversion.

This book helped me see that one of the significant things my husband and I lacked as two individuals, and definitely as a couple, was the effective ability to "recharge"—to recharge ourselves and each other. We needed to "get out of our heads," come to life, and really *live*. I'm not saying that other factors were not involved. But now I can better understand the dynamics that occurred between our personalities and our natures and be in a more informed position to learn from them.

While writing this book, I encountered personal challenges, and one had much to do with some far-reaching decisions. In fact, as I was very arduously laboring at my computer, my former husband took a new partner to be his bride. And, you know, it's funny: both his new counterpart and mine show convincing extroverted qualities, in varying degrees and depending on the situation. They are take charge, aggressive and initiating, open-up-and-spill-it-out, strongly gregarious people, in a more steady stream. Those, as described in this book, are features of their personality type. Thus, problems and conflicts also open the door to opportunities for increased self-awareness and change.

Marsha really opened up and got quite personal here, and she makes a powerful point. People need information and can use help with the things they are going through. We need to constantly search for and recognize true guidance, healthy answers, and clearer understandings. Understanding your type and the types of the important people in your life can be an invaluable tool.

The goal of this book is to initiate greater awareness—awareness of oneself and of others. Although the focus is on the workplace, these lessons really extend far beyond that, into all phases of our lives.

We heard numerous accounts of introverted adults depicting childhoods where extroverted parents who did not understand the preferences and needs of their introverted children wished for, strongly urged, pushed, and even at times forced their children to put down the books, turn off the TV, and go out and play. Introverted parents, however, can be extremely sensitive when it comes to considering the needs of their children, be they introverts or extroverts. As with everything in life, we need balance. Portia recounted some memories of her childhood with her parents:

> I think it was a valuable thing to be an introvert when I was growing up. And I'm sure my mother appreciated it. Having an introverted child, especially since I think she is an extrovert, probably made me easier to live with. Certainly I made for a calmer household, because if we had been two extroverts living together, it might have gotten a little rough at various times, especially during those teenage years. I think my dad was an introvert, though, and I was very much like him, which probably, in retrospect, may account for some of the difficulty we had in trying to communicate with each other. We were both so internal in terms of the processing we did that it was hard to get outside of our heads to talk to one another.
>
> As a mother and as an introvert, I have to find balance and learn how to reserve some of my energy for the end of the day when I'm with my son. He needs and deserves at least as much energy and intensity as I bring to the workplace. But after a long day's work, physically, my body just shuts down. So another challenge that I face is that of a

working mother who happens to also be introverted. I'm trying to work out, in my own mind, that it's OK to be at work and not always have to be in group situations. My employer may even be open to my working from home some mornings. I think that would be a good way in which I could conserve some of my energy, both for my son and for a better personal quality of life, so that I wouldn't feel so wiped out or used up by the end of the day.

Extroverts and introverts can also be sensitive to one another's needs in a marriage. Steven shared insight on his relationship with his wife:

My wife, Kelsey, is extremely extroverted, and in certain areas she has learned that there are things I really do not enjoy doing. I don't like going to the theater. So she's learned that when she wants to go to the theater, she can go with friends.

On some level it's a luxury being married to an extrovert, though, because I don't like to make plans, and she makes plans for us. She takes care of things. If she didn't make plans, I'd never get out. And once I'm there I enjoy myself—kind of. But sometimes she makes plans and I am really not in the mood for it. So there's a good side to it because I'm not alone, but there's a bad side to it, because sometimes I prefer to be alone. But when we get right down to it, I'd rather be married to an extrovert. Otherwise, I'd probably never go anywhere. I'm glad about it because it's a nice balance, although there are times when she's loaded the schedule so much even she is not so comfortable with it.

Christopher, another introvert, had this to say about his marriage:

> Initially, my wife was the social one. As an intro-
> vert, I wanted her all to myself; I didn't want to
> have to share her with anyone. I'm a performer, so
> I did enjoy the "performance" of socializing. She
> would say, "Look, we have to go and do this," and
> I would go, and "perform" a little bit. Then I would
> get my reward for being socially adept. My feeling
> of social competence is a source of gratification for
> me, rather than something that I take for granted.
> I always feel as if I have survived the interaction,
> after which I can return to my normal solitary con-
> dition. And interestingly enough, more recently, I
> have been less lethargic about initiating social
> events.

Parents, spouses, and significant others can all complement an introvert. The key is to recognize ourselves, and
understand and be flexible about the needs of those we care
about. We need to recognize the value in people and not be
quick to prejudge them. "You can observe a lot by watching"
is one of my favorite quotes from famed baseball player Yogi
Berra. We should all observe and become more informed.

Networking, Visualization, and Action

An introvert's ability to smoothly adapt to various communication styles and work environments, and to transfer their
own styles and unique gifts to many different situations, are
valuable skills. The more ease and flexibility exhibited during inner-directed (self) and outer-directed (verbal and social
interaction) communication, the greater your capacity will be

to achieve goals and seize opportunities for your fulfillment and success. If I make two phone calls, there is a potential for business. If I make zero phone calls, there is no potential for anything. That is the choice! Either you pick up the phone, or you don't. But if you don't pick up the phone, you can be certain that nothing is going to happen.

Three years ago, a colleague who was teaching a course on diversity in the graduate division of the New School for Social Research in New York asked me to be a guest speaker in one of her classes. When the students completed the requisite course work, they would move into human resource positions within various organizations. I was not going to earn any money from helping her out, but I did it anyway because I felt it was the right thing to do and I believed in the "product." Afterwards, the colleague invited all of the guest lecturers she used for that series to dinner at her house. That was a chance to meet people from organizations who were involved in diversity efforts within their own organizations. I met and got the cards of several corporate people, two of which turned into potential clients. But here's the icing on the cake: I later received four calls from the students who were in that class. These students landed jobs in major organizations that are beginning to examine diversity. Because of my lecture, those students thought of me as a conduit to get people thinking about diversity. The lecture that I gave three years ago has turned into an opportunity for me to market the products that my company now delivers. Even better, two of the companies have joined our TRENDS program (Trends in Research Evaluating New Diversity Strategies), designed to challenge the barriers to power and opportunity for a diverse workforce, both domestically and globally. The potential that exists in the marketplace has exceeded my expectations! This happened because I made myself visible. I gave a presentation to some students who remembered me and now are in a position to make a difference. It took effort, certainly, but it has also paid off. If you can get in front of an organization where you can talk about the kind of work you do, you will make invaluable networking contacts.

Are you still feeling queasy about making a presentation? Try this little exercise. Close your eyes and picture yourself talking to one person. That's it—only one. Now make eye contact with that person. Try to convince that person that your product is worth an investment. Now let's increase the number of people you are speaking with to two (don't panic!). However make eye contact with only one person at a time. Talk to one and then the other. Go from one pair of eyes to the other. Good. Now, let's increase that number from two to two thousand. It's the same concept. Think about it this way. Frank Sinatra could croon to an audience of thousands of women, yet every single woman in that audience thought his words were meant only for her because he focused on one point, either in the balcony or in the orchestra, and he sang to that point. But it appeared to the audience that he was making eye contact. The lesson here is this: If you can make eye contact with one person in a meeting, you can make eye contact with hundreds in an auditorium. The Resources section at the end of this book offers some additional resources for assistance with presentations and public speaking.

Remember, people will see you if you've done your homework. Your homework should include both those people and companies you are targeting and yourself. When formulating your actions for networking do your research, secure a suitable referral, and practice communication. Also:

1. Focus yourself with a plan. To take action, you need a *specific* plan.

2. *Do something!* If you don't take new action, nothing new will happen.

Visualization is a conscious, mental process that we all do. When we visualize our goals, we form mental pictures of our thoughts, feelings, and the things we see for ourselves. This mental visualizing helps us to clarify our thoughts and picture our direction. It's a real accomplishment when our visualized thoughts and feelings carry over into new, desired action.

Marsha Kelly visualized our collaboration. A few years ago we met, networked, and then wrote this book! We were both members of the New York Coalition of 100 Black Women, an organization of professional females. My employment committee hosted a career-management seminar, for which I did a networking presentation. Marsha was impressed. Later she approached me and mentioned how much she enjoyed and related to what I had to say. After that initial meeting, Marsha decided to join the committee, and we subsequently hosted another public "Managing Your Career" and "Networking" workshop. While waiting for our program to formally begin, she and I briefly chatted about some of the things that she does, which included her strong interest and connection with career development and management issues. During our conversation, she also mentioned that, among other things, she did proposal writing. I asked for her business card. Handing it to me, she then casually stated, "You know, I see us working together, doing something together in the near future." Marsha now relates that early on she visualized the two of us collaborating on some sort of career-strategy project. We were building our contact list, letting each other know about our skills, and, later, exploring new avenues of opportunity. Then we grabbed this opportunity found through our networking. Determining the compatibility of our individual goals, we planted the seed. It was now up to us to cultivate it.

Learning to network can become the first step toward an exciting new path. Earlier I told you about how I initially failed in my transition from the public sector to the private sector because not only did I dislike networking, I didn't even know how to do it! Even now that I've made teaching others to network my livelihood, being an introvert means I still don't necessarily enjoy it. It's easier for me to consult with my clients on a one-to-one basis, or to write this book, than to network. But I know that networking is essential to any business.

Embarking on the process of learning how to network requires courage and passion. Just as I had no idea that donating my time as a guest lecturer and the following social event would result in significant business relationships, you can never predict the value networking may have. I've found that in almost every situation where I have made the effort to network, even when I didn't want to, it has eventually paid off immeasurably for my business. And if Marsha and I hadn't set aside our introverted inclinations, we wouldn't have come together to write this book.

Understanding how introverts and extroverts communicate is important in every aspect of life. Remember to cultivate the understanding and passion it takes to make a good plan and the courage to take action. It took courage, understanding, and passion for Marsha and I to step from the well-worn paths of our lives to write this book. But these steps have developed our strengths and led us to greater realizations about ourselves. Just as in Dr. William Knaus's story from *Change Your Life Now*, which I quoted in the beginning of this book, I looked out into the mysterious shadows of the forest beyond the path, and decided to risk exploring the possibilities. It wasn't an easy decision, and it hasn't always been enjoyable, but it has enriched my life, not only in the business arena, but in the personal arena as well. Again, as Dr. Knaus wrote in his book: "Looking back on their lives, most people regret what they did not dare to do more than they regret the errors they made. And those who rarely risk anything have the most to regret" (1994).

RESOURCES

Recommended Reading

American Association of University Women. 1991. *Short-changing Girls, Shortchanging America*. Washington, D.C.: The AAUW.

Axtell, Roger. 1997. *Do's and Taboos Around the World for Women in Business*. New York: John Wiley & Sons.

Bacus, K., and J. C. Furtaw. Annual. *Asian American Information Directory*. Detroit: Gale Research, Inc.

Baldrige, Letitia. 1993. *Letitia Baldrige's New Complete Guide to Executive Manners*. New York: Scribner's.

Balzano, Frederica J. 1995. *Women, Race, Gender of Frustrator, and Reactions to Frustration*. Ann Arbor, Mich.: UMI, A Bell & Howell Information Company.

Berent, Jonathan, and Amy Lemley. 1994. *Beyond Shyness: How to Conquer Social Anxieties*. New York: Fireside/Simon & Schuster.

Bolles, Richard N. 1981. *The Three Boxes of Life*. Berkeley: Ten Speed Press.

Bolles, Richard N. Annual. *What Color Is Your Parachute?* Berkeley: Ten Speed Press.

Brennan, Gregory. 1996. *Successfully Self-Employed*. Chicago: Upstart Publishing.

Bridges, William. 1994. *Job Shift: How to Prosper in a Workplace Without Jobs*. New York: Addison-Wesley.

Bunkley, Crawford. 1996. *The African-American Network: Get Connected to More Than 5,000 Prominent People and Organizations in the African-American Community*. New York: Plume.

Burg, Bob. 1993. *Endless Referrals: Network Your Everyday Contacts into Sales*. New York: McGraw-Hill.

Cameron, Julia. 1992. *The Artist's Way*. New York: Tarcher /Putnam Penguin.

Canby, T. 1994. "In Celebration of the Good Girl." *New York Times*, September 23, A23.

Carducci, Bernard J., with Philip G. Zimbardo. 1995. "Shy?" *Psychology Today*, November–December.

Chapman, Robert, Miriam Johnson, and Robert Wegmann. 1989. *Work in the New Economy*. Indianapolis: JIST Works, Inc.

Clifford, Nancy M. 1996. "Are You an Extrovert or an Introvert?" *Teen Magazine*, July, 40, 44.

Cose, Ellis. 1993. *The Rage of a Privileged Class*. New York: Harper Collins.

Covey, Stephen R. 1989. *Seven Habits of Highly Effective People*. New York: Simon & Schuster.

Crystal, John, and Richard Bolles. 1974. *Where Do I Go from Here with My Life?* Berkeley: Ten Speed Press.

Daley, Suzanne. 1991. "Little Girls Lose Their Self Esteem On Way to Adolescence, Study Finds." *New York Times*, January 9, E4.

Dyson, Esther. 1996. "The Cyber-Maxims of Esther Dyson." *New York Times Magazine*, July 7.

Edwards, Audrey. 1997. "Essentials: LaFaye Baker, Stunt-woman." *Essence*, June.

Edwards, Audrey, and Craig Polite. 1992. *Children of the Dream*. New York: Simon & Schuster, 88.

Figler, Howard. 1988. *The Complete Job Search Handbook*. New York: Henry Holt.

Fraser, George. 1994. *Success Runs in Our Race: The Complete Guide to Effective Networking in the African-American Community*. New York: Avon Books.

Gilligan, Carol. 1982. *In a Different Voice*. Cambridge: Harvard University Press.

Granovetter, Mark. 1970. *Changing Jobs—Channels of Mobility Information in a Suburban Population*. Cambridge: Harvard University.

Gross, Kim Johnson. 1996. *Work Clothes: Casual Dress for Serious Work*. New York: Knopf.

Hakim, Cliff. 1995. *We Are All Self-Employed*. San Francisco: Berrett-Koehler.

Halfhill, Tom R. 1994. "The Introversion of America." *BYTE*, May, 278.

Heller, Bernard. 1994. *The 100 Most Difficult Business Letters You'll Ever Have to Write, Fax, or E-Mail*. New York: Harper Collins.

Henderson, Lynne, and Philip G. Zimbardo. 1998. "Shyness." *Encyclopedia of Mental Health* [On-line]. San Diego: Academic Press, www.shyness.com/encyclopedia.html.

Holtz, Herman. 1988. *How to Succeed as an Independent Consultant*. New York: John Wiley & Sons.

Holtz, Herman. 1995. *The Complete Guide to Being an Independent Contractor*. Chicago: Upstart Publishing.

Hyatt, Carole. 1995. *Lifetime Employability: How to Become Indispensable*. New York: Master Media.

Illich, Ivan. 1982. *Gender*. New York: Pantheon Books.

Johnston, D. 1990. "An Issue of Self-esteem." *New York Times*, October 4, A12.

Kalish, Karen. 1997. *How to Give a Terrific Presentation.* New York: AMACOM.

Keirsey, David, and Marilyn Bates. 1984. *Please Understand Me.* Del Mar, Calif.: Gnosology Books.

Kelley, Christopher E. 1998. *How to Be a Star at Work.* New York: Times Books.

Knaus, William J. 1994. *Change Your Life Now: Powerful Techniques for Positive Change.* New York: John Wiley & Sons.

Kotter, John P. 1983. Self-Assessment Exercises. Developed for his Power Dynamics classes at Harvard Business School.

Kroeger, O., and J. Thuesen. 1994. *Type Talk at Work.* New York: Dell.

Lawrence, Gordon. 1982. *People Types and Tiger Stripes.* Gainesville: Center for Applications of Psychological Type.

Mathis, Darlene. 1994. *Women of Color: The Multicultural Guide to Fashion and Beauty.* New York: Ballantine.

McCormick, Neil. 1998. "Born to Be Mild, Actually." *The Daily Telegraph*, May 16, D5.

Morning Edition. 1998. With Duncan Watts, Steven Strogatz, and Jim Collins interviewed by David Baron. NPR. WNYC, New York. June 4.

Morning Edition. 1995. With Philip G. Zimbardo interviewed by Alex Chadwick. NPR. WNYC, New York. August 30.

Morrison, Ann, Randall P. White, Ellen VanVelsor, and Center for Creative Leadership. 1992. *Breaking the Glass Ceiling.* Reading, Mass.: Addison-Wesley.

Morrison, Terri. 1994. *Kiss, Bow, or Shake Hands: How to Do Business in Sixty Countries.* Holbrook, Mass.: Bob Adams.

Myers, Isabel Briggs, and Mary H. McCaulley. 1988. *A Guide to the Development and Use of the Myers-Briggs Type Indicator.* Palo Alto: Consulting Psychologists Press.

Myers, Isabel Briggs, and Peter B. Myers. 1980. *Gifts Differing.* Palo Alto: Consulting Psychologists Press.

Myers-Briggs Type Indicator. 1977. Palo Alto: Consulting Psychologists Press.

O'Connor, Regis. 1997. *High Impact Public Speaking for Business and the Professions.* Lincolnwood, Ill.: Ntc/ Contemporary Publishing Group.

Oldenburg, Ray. 1997. *The Great Good Place: Cafes, Coffee Shops, Community Centers, Beauty Parlors, General Stores, Bars, Hangouts and How They Get You Through the Day.* New York: Marlowe & Co.

Parker, Sheila, Mimi Nichter, Mark Nichter, Nancy Vuckovic, Collette Sims, and Cheryl Ritenbaugh. 1994. *Body Image and Weight Concerns Among African American and White Adolescent Females: Differences Which Make a Difference.* Tucson: University of Arizona.

Rifkin, Jeremy. 1995. *The End of Work: The Decline of the Global Labor Force and the Dawn of the Post-Market Era.* New York: G. P. Putnam's Sons.

RoAne, Susan. 1993. *The Secrets of Savvy Networking.* New York: Warner.

Rowan, Carl. 1991. *Breaking Barriers.* New York: Little, Brown.

Schneir, Franklin, and Lawrence Welkowitz. 1996. *The Hidden Face of Shyness: Understanding and Overcoming Social Anxiety.* New York: Avon.

Sher, Barbara. 1986. *Wishcraft: How to Get What You Really Want.* New York: Ballantine.

Sher, Barbara. 1995. *I Could Do Anything If Only I Knew What It Was.* New York: Bantam Doubleday Dell.

Shinn, Florence Scovell. 1979. *The Game of Life and How to Play It.* Marina del Rey, Calif.: Devorss Publications.

Slater, Philip. 1976. *The Pursuit of Loneliness.* Boston: Beacon Press.

Tieger, Paul D., and Barbara Barron-Tieger. 1995. *Do What You Are: Discover the Perfect Career for You Through the Secrets of Personality Type, Second Edition.* Boston: Little Brown.

Tieger, Paul D., and Barbara Barron-Tieger. 1993. *The Personality Type Tool Kit.* San Jose: Communication Consultants.

Timm, Paul R. 1992. *Basics of Oral Communication: Skills for Career and Personal Growth.* Cincinnati, Ohio: South-Western.

Timm, Paul R. 1997. *Winning Telephone Tips: 30 Fast and Profitable Tips for Making the Best Use of Your Phone.* Hawthorne, N.J.: Career Press.

Tuller, Lawrence. 1993. *Doing Business in Latin America and the Caribbean.* New York: AMACOM.

Tullier, Michelle. 1997. *Cover Letters (Job Search Series).* New York: Princeton Review and Random House.

Tullier, Michelle L. 1998. *Networking for Everyone.* Indianapolis: JIST Works, Inc.

Uchitelle, Louis, and N. R. Kleinfield. 1996. "The Downsizing of America." *New York Times,* March 3–9, 1.

Wendelton, Kate. 1992. *Through the Brick Wall.* New York: Villard Books.

Wendelton, Kate. 1997. *Targeting the Job You Want.* New York: Five O'Clock Club Books.

Yamada, Haru. 1997. *Different Games, Different Rules: Why Americans and Japanese Misunderstand Each Other.* New York: Oxford University Press.

Zimbardo, Philip. 1990. *Shyness: What It Is, What to Do About It.* Reading, Mass.: Addison-Wesley.

Presentations and Public Speaking: Where to Go for Help

Applied Behavioral Technologies
201-439-1609

Dale Carnegie Courses
800-342-7787

Decker Communications
800-547-0050

The Executive Speaker
561-664-5256

The Executive Technique
312-266-0001

Fred Pryor Seminars
800-255-6139

Toastmasters International
800-993-7732

World Wide Web Job Search Advice and Job Listings

America's Job Bank
www.ajb.dni.us:80/

The Black Collegian Online
www.black-collegian.com

Career America
www.careeramerica.com

Career Center for Workforce Diversity
www.eop.com

Career City
www.careercity.com

Career Consultants
www.personalitytype.com

Career Magazine
www.careermag.com

Career Mosaic
www.careermosaic.com

Career Path
www.careerpath.com

CAREERXROADS
www.careerxroads.com

Drake Beam Morin
www.dbm.com/

Eagleview
www.eagleview.com

Latino Web
www.catalog.com/favision/latnoweb

The Monster Board
www.monster.com

ABOUT THE AUTHOR

Dr. Frederica Balzano is the founder and president of Effective Management Resources, Inc. EMR, a consulting firm dedicated to assisting human resource and senior management professionals, teaches the techniques to develop the right people with the right skills for the right job, thereby maintaining an effective, productive, and committed workforce. Managing a staff that is as diverse as the products EMR offers, Fredi's expertise lies in leadership development, executive assessment and coaching, career management and transition counseling, and diversity. EMR works with Partners in Human Resources International, LLC, around issues of assessment and diversity.

Fredi is recognized as a highly compelling and motivated speaker. Her training seminars have been utilized by many organizations including Citicorp/Citibank, Revlon, and Major League Baseball. Her design of the award-winning program Networking for Introverts©, the only seminar of its kind on the market, has been hailed for effecting real change for individuals and organizations as they interact with today's changing business environments. Heavily researched, Networking for Introverts© explores the myths of introversion and gives participants a model to use in becoming more effective in an extroverted workforce. This increases both individual and organizational effectiveness.

Fredi also designed a program for the high-potential or high-performing executive who may need development in one or more career management areas. The focus of this program is to help participants achieve and maintain excellent work performance within the complexities of organizational changes. Utilizing enhanced 360° feedback and/or Benchmarks®, clients will confirm their current career direction, find possible new directions to consider, or find ways to improve a job that has become routine or is no longer a good fit. Executive Coaching can be tailored to the needs of mid-level employees wishing to join the senior managerial team; it can also be used with survivors of downsizings, restructurings, and mergers and acquisitions who are faced with the issues of effectively managing a career in a new environment.

Fredi created the TRENDS program (Trends in Research Evaluating New Diversity Strategies), a strategic forum designed to inform and assist organizations in managing the cross-cultural and diversity issues present in the global workplace.

Fredi holds both a Ph.D. and a master's degree in psychology from New York University. She is a member of the Financial Women's Association, the Association of Black Women in Higher Education, and the National Coalition of 100 Black Women. She serves on the board of directors for the New York chapter of the International Association of Career Management Professionals and the Double Discovery Center at Columbia University. She is a member of The Alumni Board of New York University, and the board of the Jose Limón Dance Company. Fredi is also a Fellow on the International Board for Career Management Certification.

An original Brooklyn girl and Brooklyn Dodger fan, Fredi lives in New York City and gardens on Shelter Island.